Under Her Skin

How Girls Experience Race in America

edited by Pooja Makhijani

SEAL PRESS

Published by
Seal Press
An Imprint of Avalon Publishing Group, Incorporated
1400 65th Street, Suite 250
Emeryville, CA 94608

Library of Congress Cataloging-in-Publication Data

Under her skin : how girls experience race in America / [edited] by Pooja Makhijani.
     p. cm.
  ISBN 1-58005-117-0
  1. Race awareness in children—United States. 2. Girls—United States—Psychology. I. Makhijani, Pooja.

BF723.R3U53 2004
305.235'2'089—dc22

                                            2004019803

9 8 7 6 5 4 3 2 1

Cover Design: Diane Rigoli
Interior Design: Margaret Copeland/Terragrafix
Printed in the United States of America by Worzalla
Distributed by Publishers Group West

*You never really understand a person until
you consider things from his point of view . . .
until you climb into his skin and walk around in it.*

— Atticus to Scout in Harper Lee's
To Kill a Mockingbird

Table of Contents

Introduction

Pooja Makhijani

There was only one other Indian child in my third-grade class—a Sikh boy whose name I can't remember. His mother, who must have been very loving and attentive, knotted his hair into a neat bun and covered it in a patka, the baby turban he would wear until he graduated to a full turban. His patka always matched his clothes; he even had a denim one for when he wore jeans to school.

There were clear disadvantages to there being only two of "us," especially since he was a boy and I was a girl. I let the playground chants of "Pooja and His Name, sitting in a tree, K-I-S-S-I-N . . ." go in one ear and out the other. I shrugged when girls asked me whether I *liked* him. I never, ever put his name on my list of boys when we played MASH.

I should have defended him on the blacktop that day when a boy pulled off his coordinated patka. He was rounding second base during the daily kickball game at recess when a pale hand yanked the swatch of red fabric off his head. His silky black locks cascaded down his shoulders. A few kids gathered around and one even yelled, "He's a girl!" But he just snatched his patka back and went inside. When he showed up in class after recess was over, almost everyone looked up from his or her Sustained Silent Reading. I didn't, but instead snuck a glance in his direction at the end of the period. His patka was lopsided and haphazard; the school nurse wouldn't have known how to retie it.

That day, I didn't speak up for him. What would I have said? What could I have said? At that age, it's each one for herself. No one wants to draw attention for being even the least bit different. I was also in my I-refuse-to-be-Indian-how-can't-you-see-that-I-am-as-white-as-you phase: declining to participate in International Day, throwing away Indian lunches that my mother carefully packed for me, wondering how I could change my name to something less conspicuous, like Melissa. In our school, white was "cool." And desirable. Like Michelle, whose lustrous white-blonde hair was referred to as "corn silk" by our second-grade teacher. Or Patrick, who was always picked first when we played softball in gym class. Or James, who had magical birthday parties at the ice-skating rink, with generous goody bags, dressed-up Disney characters on skates, and more candy than you could collect for Halloween.

By fifth grade, there were seven South Asian kids in my elementary school. That was in 1989, after the passage of the Immigration Reform and Control Act, which removed country quotas and educational and professional requirements for immigrants to the United States. Quintessential New Jersey suburbs like mine—with Elks Lodges, Girl Scout troops, soccer leagues, church fairs, and post–World War II prefabricated houses constructed from one set of plans in row after row, even to the placement of a tree in exactly the same place in every yard—became home to thousands of immigrants from India.

We were still matched up: With five girls and two boys, there were just more combinations. So we avoided each other at school. But we were invited to each other's birthday parties, where we played Pin the Tail on the Donkey and bobbed for apples, devoured Hot Mix and samosas, and ate lots and lots of cake.

In *Bird by Bird: Some Instructions on Writing and Life,* Anne Lamott tells her students to "start with your childhood. . . . Plug your nose and jump in, and write down all your memories as truthfully as you can." She goes on to tell readers that Flannery O'Connor once said that "anyone who survived childhood has enough material to write for the rest of his or her life."

When, eleven years after leaving elementary school, I embarked on my own writing career, I remembered Lamott's advice and furiously wrote down anything and everything I could recall. I often ended up recounting my memories about race.

I wrote about an incident that occurred when I was in first grade. We all walked into the classroom one morning and my teacher saw that a swastika had been spray-painted on the window the night before. Harried and hurried, she called the janitor to remove the offending mark. When several students asked her about it, she distracted them, perhaps with a math problem or an art project. Granted, we were in first grade and didn't have the capacity to learn about the rise and fall of the Third Reich, but a simple history lesson may have eased the unvoiced tension in the room.

I wrote about the racism of many of my parents' Indian friends. When I was old enough to refill the chutney and kebabs on their cocktail plates, but still too young to sit with them at dinner, I would catch snippets of their whispered side conversations: "She married a *white* boy." "We were thinking about moving there. But there were some *Mexicans* in the neighborhood." "They just promoted him because he was *black*."

I wrote about how the heady scent of cloves, cumin, and cardamom from my mother's kitchen seeped into my clothes. While my brown-skinned family and friends told me I smelled like "something good to eat," my classmates found it unpleasant. I was twelve years old when Jimmy told me that I "totally smelled," and perhaps, at that age, I was dealing with other "growing up" issues that made the incident particularly painful. It took me days to write down those two words he had said. In the end, I closed my eyes and typed them, thinking that if I didn't look at the words, no one else could see them either.

꧁꧂

It was this last piece of writing that inspired me to pursue this project. I emailed an early draft to a dear college friend and told him how difficult it was to produce. But after reliving the experience a half-dozen times through writing it, and being courageous enough to share it with my writing group, I realized that I felt better, and stronger, about what had happened (however minor it had been). It gave me an avenue to talk about race with people around me in places I felt it wasn't usually discussed: over dinner with a bunch of girl-friends, at family functions, or in otherwise quotidian Instant-Messenger conversations.

I discovered that folks were overflowing with stories to share because they had never had the opportunity to do so before. And I then knew I wanted to create a space—a safe, artistic place—where those childhood moments could be shared, questioned, analyzed, forgiven.

I admit I did have a bias as I read through the hundreds of submissions I received: I was most interested in those child-hood experiences that spoke of histories—personal, communal, national—and found those essays that confronted the intersection between history and memory to be the most compelling. These essays made me feel like I was on a journey —to search for the meaning in those facts. In the most successful pieces, the essayist went beyond the simple autobiographical chronologies and history book dates; she created a union between inside and outside. The best pieces were transcendent: An essay is an exploration of self; ultimately, a writer cannot understand the world without analyzing herself, and she cannot discover herself without probing the world.

The qualities I admire most about the essays that I finally selected, aside from being exquisitely crafted, are their authenticity and honesty. In reading an essay, I want to feel that I'm engaged with a person who is real, who makes mistakes and learns from them. This is cliché, I know, but it is very difficult to find. The ideal personal essay is not static, but an undulating piece of art that is deep and thought-provoking. It should crest and break in different patterns each time you read it.

I received many inquiries from men wanting to submit— they wrote to me that I was being unfair, discriminatory, and told me that my anthology would be incomplete without their voices. Absolutely, this collection would be different if their points of view were included. Women and men do have different childhood experiences: Girls more than boys, I think, deal with issues such as self-confidence and body image, cliques, and definitions of gender roles. My aim in collecting these stories was to showcase the depth and breadth of women's experiences.

Many writer friends asked me how I would keep the book's tone from being one of bitterness and blame or how this anthology could avoid ending up a series of tirades on "how much it sucks to be excluded when you really wanted to fit in." When I conceived of this book, I wanted it to be about strength. It is hard to face, head-on, childhood experiences; they are always formative and lasting. It takes a special courage to reveal, in art, the racism of your parents or the physical violence you suffered at the hands of your classmates or that you inflicted on others.

I always wanted to write about my Sikh classmate. It is one of those memories whose sounds and colors don't fade away with time. I often imagine an alternate ending: I could have brought the situation to the attention of an otherwise-engaged lunch aide or trusted teacher; I could have accompanied him to the nurse's office and made sure he called his mother to come help him put his patka on correctly; I could have faced those boys—told them I thought they were being really mean. I think how wonderful it might be if he picks up this book, reads the introduction, and realizes that there was someone thinking about him that day on the blacktop.

I make no claim that these essays are representative of the diversity of race and racism in the United States: Even after combing through the overwhelming number of submissions

I received and soliciting pieces from writers I admired, I am sure that I may have missed something, viewpoints I did not consider. All I can say is that I liked these essays a lot; they made me think, and they got under my skin. I hope that as you read this collection of essays, and admire the candor and courage in these pieces, you might pick up a pen or sit down at the computer and add on your own story.

Becoming

Anita Darcel Taylor

Rain dampened the schoolyard, the soft, warm kind that entices children to play harder, faster, more competitively in hopes of beating it back. The white chipped paint of the baseball diamond blended into asphalt gray. And the games went on. *Pop!* The baseball against the wood of the bat. *Flash!* The ball, flying overhead. Tiny figures scrambled in the outfield, past the jungle gym, past the hopscotch squares, past the stand-alone army-metal slide that reached eight feet into the sky, past me, the chunky five-year-old standing under rushing clouds waiting for the rains to come. Did the other kids realize that clouds were galloping like horses overhead? Did they know that rain would come and maybe lightning and thunder and when they did, the lightning and the thunder, there would be nowhere to lie down and be still until it passed over? "Hush until God's work is done," Grandma Sue said. I don't think they cared, those kids with their baseball mitts and chipped-tooth grins.

I didn't belong there, in that red-brick school filled with kids of all sizes, kids who moved in clumps of plaid skirts and gray, blue, and brown trousers, kids with silken blond, brown, and red hair. My brother went to school there, too. I was in kindergarten and he was in third grade. On the walk home on my first day of school, he abandoned me and I never really saw him at school again. I found my way home alone to our new house—138 Elm Street—six blocks or so from Brandywine Elementary School. My landmark was the big yellow house on the corner of Elm and Becker, the Daleys' house. Once I was in front of it I knew to head uphill, that halfway up the climb was the brown, shingled, two-story house that was ours. Having made it on my own that first afternoon, I was on my own every day thereafter.

I liked our house, not so much because my parents owned it but because we truly lived in it, legs flopped over the living room sofa, rings from soda glasses' condensation on the coffee table, nicks and scars and Wrigley's chewing gum stuck to headboards and under tables. I didn't know anything about the petition to get rid of us, the blacks. I was protected from all of that.

Being an only daughter, I didn't share my bedroom, the bigger one at the back, off the kitchen. The walls were yellow-wallpapered, unmistakably a girl's room, with one yellow-laced window curtain that stayed closed to the neighbors' driveway. The window was sealed shut. Later, when I was older, I wrote in there, in that solitary space of my own, in the ninety-five-cent pastel-colored plastic diaries I bought at Clark's Five and Ten on State Street next to the library. And I spent hours reading the tomboy antics of Trixie Belden and Honey Wheeler, prissy Nancy Drew and her crew far too pedestrian for my tastes.

But I'm getting ahead of myself. I wasn't reading Trixie in kindergarten, not on the day I stood in the schoolyard watching the baseball game, waiting for the rains to come. I was reading. To teach me the ABCs when I was three, my father used the black Remington manual typewriter my mother bought for typing lessons—she wanted to be our church's secretary. By age four, I was reading and writing simple words. I don't remember not being able to read, even if I thought it was "iz-land" instead of "island." I knew what it meant in the sentence. It meant a comfortable, faraway place where one could be alone.

My teachers worried about me and my desire for seclusion. They thought it was a sign of something deeper. Their progress reports noted that I was a fine student, bright and helpful; marks of "outstanding" appear next to most of my subjects. But always a caveat: "Is something going on at home? She's a very sensitive child. And shy. She cries very easily. And the stories she writes, always about her mother. Is everything okay?" Nothing was wrong at home. My parents were tender; Daddy never left the house before kissing Mommy and me. Mommy rarely left the house without me in tow.

My mother worked the night shift as a nurse's aide at the Catholic hospital one block away, where I was born. My

father worked as a bricklayer or cook during the day, the bru-
tality of New York seasons dictating which. My brother and I
were always cared for by loving if extremely tired parents.
Still, it was true, I was a sensitive child, insecure, wheezing
and coughing and shuttled to the doctor for shots or to the
hospital for air. Always needing more.

It wasn't that I necessarily wanted to be alone. Even as I
walked to and from school with the stones I kicked as company, I wondered what it might be like to be someone else,
someone with hordes of friends, someone typical or average.
But I chose the quiet of the library to the noise of anticipated
rejection at recess, or I cozied up as teacher's pet. Teachers
rarely reject an attentive child. Even now I wonder what Ms.
Romeo must have thought at camp that weekend when I was
eight, my refusing to hike with the other kids or jump on the
trampoline, but instead staying by her side helping prepare
meals or hunting kindling for the fire. She let me sleep in the
bunk next to hers each night, me in my big pink hair curlers
and fluffy robe, stuffed inside a Girl Scout–green sleeping bag.
Nine years later, I ran into her in Linton High School's hallway. She called my name, my full name, and smiled. I remembered her, too. She looked exactly the same as she did those
mornings I woke up with my pink hair curlers still in place,
volunteering my services for the day.

I knew I was an odd little girl. Just as I stood watching
from the fence behind the baseball diamond, I treated child-

hood as a spectator sport. The sidelines are a fascinating place for a little girl with wide eyes.

Each Sunday, I sat in the dining room with my father as my mother bathed and dressed for church. Daddy had already dressed me, shined my shoes, braided my hair, tied the bow on the back of my cotton A-line dress so that the loops were even and the flaps fell wide. We sat at the dining room table listening not to the Christian music of a typical Baptist Sunday, but to Daddy's church music: John Coltrane, Charlie Parker, Miles Davis, Dinah Washington, and Aretha Franklin. I especially liked Aretha. With her I could sing and tap my foot; dancing was not allowed in our house on Sundays. I didn't know what Aretha meant by "laughing on the outside, crying on the inside," but I knew her effect. My feet tapped and my spirit swayed in a rhythm complementary to her sadness, full and wide and deep and maybe just a little bit familiar. I liked Aretha, and so did Daddy. His foot tapped, too, as he watched Mommy peacock back and forth from their bedroom to the bathroom, once in just her panties and a bra, then panties, bra, and sheer black stockings, then panties, bra, stockings, and girdle, and so on until in full dress and full makeup she transformed from the Monday-through-Saturday Mommy to the Sunday woman of God. Daddy and I loved it when she was a woman because she was beautiful, and I wanted to look like her, too, and make a grown-up man's foot tap to Aretha Franklin and smile.

"Ump, I sure didn't marry her for her breasts," he said beneath his breath as his eyes moved past that near-flat top, lowering to the hugeness of her buttocks as she passed us and passed us and passed us again. I'd no clue what he meant, but I knew that gazing at the bold, wide, round butt that was my mother's, Daddy smiled and was very happy. My mother had Saartjie's ass, the ass of the Hottentot Venus. And for that Daddy was extremely grateful. Mommy never complained about the size of her butt, although I suspect she knew Daddy liked it, so tended to wear the tailored clothes that flattered without accentuating, adding a flair of mystery and fantastic imagination for men not as lucky as her husband.

I wanted to be like my mom when I grew up: tiny waist and flat tummy, petite breasts that didn't bounce around even when she didn't wear a bra, which was most of the time as she drank pots of coffee while talking endless hours with friends, living the leisure life of the working poor where the community you make is the key to your bounty. But already family was telling me that I was just like my father—tall with big, heavy, muscular legs. Daddy had the wide back and broad, round shoulders of a construction worker, but his fingers, his fingers were long and delicate, always perfectly manicured— the hands of a surgeon or a writer.

Once, rummaging through my mother's belongings, I found a box, a small wooden box with a camel-hump top. It smelled of cedar when opened; it smelled old. I liked the smell of old, and on extra-quiet days, sad days, I sat in the corner of my parents' bedroom, lifted the box from the bottom dresser drawer and smelled it. It took me a while to gain the courage to open the letters inside, bundled in a ribbon, twenty or so. They were letters to my mother, written in black ink, letters with words that looked like pictures. Calligraphy? They were letters from my father, written from strange places like Okinawa and San Francisco, written when they were dating, between 1950 and 1952. They were love letters.

I likened myself to him, my dad. I wanted to know how to write pretty letters that boys would wrap in bows. I wanted to know how to make the house smell like Sunday dinner, how to make flowers grow, and how to dance. These were the delicate things he did, the soft things. But he did hard things, too. He laid brick and climbed scaffolds and poured concrete and made houses. Yet still his belly jiggled, a big, flabby belly that, when he wasn't suited and tied, hung over the belt of his pants and jiggled when he laughed. That would be the thing I inherited, instantly, even at five years old, a jiggling belly—not pretty words or yummy foods or flower pots, but a jiggling belly that bubbled over everything and made kids call me fat. "That's you when you grow up, Anita," my mother teased as my father sat shirtless and jelly-bellied on the sofa watching football, sipping Scotch. "Ugh," I thought, and retreated to my bedroom.

However fat he was, though, my father could dance, graceful and smooth—with women other than my mother, because she had no rhythm for dancing—as if the music flowed up through him, creating sound through movement instead of through cold woofers and tweeters. This, the gift I craved, to be brave enough to own the dance floor, would elude me, too. In this one area, social ability, I would come nowhere near to emulating Dad.

Instead I was shy, stereotypically, painfully shy, clinging to the fence. I was too afraid to ask to join in, even though batting practice alone in my yard assured me that I could hit one easily out past the right-field kid with the glasses and the too-new mitt. I wanted to play. I wanted badly to play. But instead I clung to the fence, as invisible as a chubby young girl, tall for her age, in short braids and gray orthopedic shoes, holding an adult's black umbrella, could be.

Next to me stood Jackie, leaning against the wire fence, serenely engaged in a book—not a picture book but a real one—oblivious to the ballgame going on without either of us. Jackie Spain was in each one of my classes, from kindergarten to our elementary school graduating year, the year Richard Nixon beat the pants off Hubert Humphrey to claim the White House, the year Douglas Vonie left Brandywine Elementary, the year I said goodbye to so many things.

Our pairing was Principal Vonie's doing—two little girls in need of friendship, one black, one white, in a time when the nation was desperate, too, for similar union. Principal Vonie was a big man, tall and trim but wide, with imposing shoulders and a shock of thick hair that I remember as stark, cold black and my mother as flaming red. He's in his eighties now, sick and a little frail but still with a massive frame and imposing manner, still inquiring of mutual friends about my whereabouts and probably Jackie's, too.

Jackie and I were opposites. She was petite; I was large. Her brown, thick, silken hair was long to my short, coarse braids; her skin the color of cold buttermilk to my hot-cocoa complexion. Was she shy or did she simply prefer her own company? There was nothing about Jackie that suggested she wanted to be asked to play baseball. She seemed content to stand unfettered by the fence with an open book and a closed umbrella. What was her secret?

At age five, I had not yet considered the strangeness of race, its invisibility in my new friendship with Jackie. It was the '60s and I was in Schenectady, away from the South, away from the city, miles away from the hosing of nonviolence. And yet I had an inkling that there was something, some odd thing about me that made a little boy trip me on the way from school one day, splattering my books all over the wet ground, laughing as he and his bigger friends yelled "nigger" before running away. Jackie never called me that.

Over our six-year friendship, I spent a lot of nights at the Spains'. Unlike my mother, who worked the hospital graveyard shift with rarely a weekend off, Jackie's mother worked the regular hours of a businesswoman—maybe she was a secretary—and so had time to help us pull chocolate taffy from one side of the kitchen to the other on Saturday afternoons or plant tiny marigolds in the backyard garden after the sun went down. The flowers looked like miniature suns themselves. We ate dinners as a family at the dining room table—spaghetti was a favorite—and we talked mostly about school or other things routine in the daily lives of the Spains. With them life was easy, almost simple, like nothing mattered except the moment we were in. The world did not seep into the little Spain house on Becker Street.

But behind Jackie's bedroom door, it was different. In the four-walled capsule that was her private room, I entered a private space of my own. On the floor next to her bookshelf I sat, legs crossed, envying her collection of little-girl mysteries, her solitude, her indifference about being asked to play baseball. I fingered the spines of her books, picking them up and flipping through, reading a line here, a paragraph there, considering them the way one does at a library or bookstore. With which would I spend the next few hours? I handled them as if they were hungry baby birds; if I were not careful, they might disappear from my grasp and I would be left with only the memory of sights unseen, visions lost, perished, mouths still opened. In my memories, Jackie is barely there. It is me on the floor with her books, surrounded by sunshiny yellow walls and girlish lace: me alone, wishing that this was my bedroom and these were my books.

I wonder now why it is that I have so much difficulty conjuring up specific moments of our young life together. After all, our social lives were completely intertwined and yet the memories come so slowly.

At ten years old, we spent our first weeks away from home at Camp Kawankomi in Lake George, where Jackie taught me about fossils and poison ivy and the different types of trees all with different kinds of leaves, which we picked from the ground and slipped into envelopes for safekeeping. We played long and hard that first day at camp until, by the day's end, we both smelled silvery from sweat, not at all minding that the shower water was ice cold, waiting hungrily for our turn to wash the metallic smell away.

"You have to wash your hair too, Anita," she said as I reached for my plastic shower cap.

"But I can't, Jackie. I just had it done. Mom said not to unbraid my hair and, when I was in water, wear the shower cap or the bathing cap."

"But your hair will smell funny if you don't wash it," she insisted and so I did. I unraveled my braids and stood under the cold shower, borrowing her shampoo and scrubbing until my hands against my scalp made a squeaking sound, which Jackie said meant that my hair was now clean.

We dried ourselves and slipped into our pajamas and robes, walked back to our lean-to, a little three-sided log cabin with a roof and wide-open front. Jackie's brown hair fell smooth down her back, but all the straightness washed out of mine as soon as the water hit. I had a mound of black puff all over my head. "What are we going to do with your hair now, Anita? It's not straight anymore."

"We can try to braid it, I guess. Do you know how?" I asked, hoping she'd answer yes.

"I think so," she said and she sat me down on the edge of her cot as she stood beside me, combing and brushing and twisting my mass into three big bumps that held themselves together only temporarily, but it was good enough and we giggled about the mess we made before curling up side by side into a summer's sleep in view of all the ferns and oaks and elms she'd taught me about that day. We both smelled delicious. Following breakfast the next morning we ran to the lake, where we held hands and jumped in over our heads, me as free as Jackie, my bathing cap back on my bed.

The outside world flooded into our house on Elm Street. We felt the shadow of conflict—Vietnam, civil rights, feminism, the Bible. Mom and Dad had no use for television if it was not to watch the news. We celebrated the day presidential candidate Bobby Kennedy visited Brandywine on his campaign trail. The first time I saw my mother cry was the day Martin Luther King, Jr., was killed. She hid in the pantry and tried to collect herself. She failed. "What is going to happen to us now?" my father asked God, shaking his head as if denying the piercing stab of it. We watched Walter Cronkite report on the Vietnam conflict (when did we start calling it a war?) on the little black-and-white television set that Mom or Dad wheeled into the kitchen each evening at suppertime. Our usually chatty selves were quiet then, as if we were in church. The gospel was being delivered.

In those days, too, feminism had momentum, as did hatred for Lyndon Johnson. Rhetoric reigned. "A woman needs a man like a fish needs a bicycle!" shouted Gloria Steinem. "Build a great society!" begged Johnson. Conscientious objectors headed north. Johnson's presidency crumbled. "Say it loud, I'm black and I'm proud," sang a sweaty, processed James Brown. Black Power rumbled, and Uncle Tom became the antichrist. I worried. My only friend was white.

Brandywine Elementary School did not reflect Schenectady's ethnic ratio, where Italians dominated the Irish, Polish, and blacks. Hamilton Hill was home to most poor blacks, and most of us blacks were poor—working and prideful, but poor just the same. Most of Brandywine's grade school students attended what is now named Martin Luther King Jr. Elementary School—Schenectady parroting other cities, identifying schools with the poorest, blackest bodies and branding them King. Brandywine was overwhelmingly white. Blacks attended the school across town on Hamilton Hill. So when Linda Williams brought Hamilton Hill to Brandywine, tall and slender with a skin tone and red hair like Malcolm X's, she seemed exotic. Linda did not spend her Saturdays at O'Dell Loveless's beauty parlor getting her hair fried, twisted, and curled to mock the white girls on the cover of *Seventeen* magazine. Linda looked like a miniature Angela Davis with a bush that bent gracefully to the wind without ever losing its form. A bush was a political statement, symbolic of a certain belonging, a secret knowing. I wanted that, too.

There was a certain clubbiness among Brandywine's black population. Most of its members were older than I, but not by much, a year or two, except for my brother, who was three years older and seemed a bit of a ringleader. Lots of the kids came to my house after school to sit all over the bed and on the floor of my brother's bedroom, a place forbidden to me, and listen to records on his private record player. They listened sometimes to James Brown, but mostly they played strange stuff from musical groups called the Last Poets and Gil Scott-Heron and the Revolution. I was jealous of them all. I could hear them laughing and talking about things I knew nothing of. But mostly it hurt not to be invited. There were girls there and boys; some of the girls were even my age. Linda Williams and Terri Jo and a girl named Rena, who became my brother's girlfriend. I remember her clearly because when someone pointed out to her that I was his sister, I heard her laugh, "That fat girl? Damn, she's ugly!" Jackie never noticed that I was fat. And she never said anything about me being ugly. At Jackie's house, I was normal.

It was Terri Jo who gave me the ultimatum. "Drop the white girl, Anita, or else," and I complied like Jackie was yesterday's newspaper. Each morning when Jackie knocked on my door to join me in the half-block walk to the new territory of junior high, I pretended I wasn't yet dressed, sending her on her way alone until finally she stopped knocking. We passed one another in the halls unacknowledged. She walked alone for a short time, and then I thought I saw her holding a boy's hand. Maybe she wasn't, but they were definitely walking through the halls together between each class period. Jackie had a friend. I, on the other hand, did not. I had misinterpreted Terri Jo's ultimatum. I thought that in exchange for Jackie I was being offered membership in the black group, but I was no more or less black than I had been in sixth grade. And I belonged to nothing.

Solace came in singing, lending my alto to the chorus. Foreign phrases found a home in my voice. Loneliness stuck there, too. Outside the music room I longed for Jackie, but she obeyed my earlier silent pronouncement and left me to my blackness. The wall between us was stronger than stone.

From an awkward distance I watched Linda Williams and her friends enjoy cliquish exclusivity. She admired my purse once, a suede satchel with a long wide strap that made it hit softly against my hip. It had fringes over the flap, and when I carried it I felt western, ancient, native, cool. It was a gift and I adored it. In it I carried a small book or two, asthma medications, my diary, a picture of my dad when he was young and healthy and handsome. Linda adored it, too, and asked to borrow it. Could defying my mother's rule against loaning clothing mean that Linda and I would be friends? I took my chances and loaned it to her. She never gave it back. I never mustered the courage to ask. She carried it until it was no longer a soft calf brown but a slick, ink-stained dirt color. I told my mother I lost it.

The purse opened no doors. Linda and her friends attended parties in one another's living rooms and concerts at Union College and Albany State. They talked in a slang that felt foreign in my mouth. They wore the fashions of slim girls with round hips, while I still wore orthopedic shoes and dressed from women's boutiques in women's sizes. And I watched.

I watched the white students, too, board buses for Vermont's Mount Snow, wishing that my lungs would stop rebelling and allow me to experience the frosted air of New England's downhill skiing. Sometimes a group allowed me a visit and I entered, hopeful that my membership would be lifetime. It never was. Instead I was welcomed among a small group of misfits. Those included Emily and Michael, a white girl and a black boy, dating each other and angry, Emily routinely swallowing fists full of Bayer aspirin as an indication of her suffering, protesting silly things like not being allowed to bring her black boyfriend home to her white parents' dinner table. Once, as a joke, Emily's friends pushed Michael and me into a broom closet, barricading the door behind us. "Blacks should date blacks," they chanted. Michael and I stood frozen in place, the room so dark we could not see our own hands, let alone one another's face. We were perfectly still until, finally, the door was opened and we rushed out, gobbling air. Both of us must have been holding our breath, so frightening was the prospect of being together alone. The group soon dispersed, patting Michael on the back as if he'd accomplished a colossal feat, having shared moments alone in the closet with me. Girls and boys all, they left together, laughing. Even Emily. I stood there in the hallway alone, for a very long time, trying not to cry.

"Aren't you going to burn yours?" a boy asked, never once lowering his head to peek at my troublesomely bulbous teenaged breasts. I was fourteen years old.

Irritation erupted and I turned to stare down this stupid black child who ought to have known better. "Do you have any idea how much my mother pays for these things?" was the answer I offered. His was the only other black face in the crowd.

He pulled his bike to mine, and together we watched and listened as radical white women shouted about breaking the shackles of men, housewifery, and of all things, bras. "Free your breasts and proclaim your independence." They pranced around a barrel drum filled with flame, fueled by cotton and nylon, metal clips and stays rebelling against the burn. What were we doing here, two black kids, barely teens, witnessing this display of displaced activism? "Do you think these women actually know any black women who don't work?" I asked him.

"Do you think these women know any black women at all?" he retorted. I looked at him, looked at the crowd of white women, the absence of black. There we were on Hamilton Hill watching white beg for the attention of black.

Every city, every town, has a Hamilton Hill, that place of "other." Across the tracks, on the outskirts of town, in the ghetto, the barrio, or slum. Every town has its other, the place outside the interior world, where dual identities are required: the one that is and the one that is accepted. I used to sneak to Hamilton Hill often on my bicycle—it was a territory forbidden by my parents.

It was Saturday morning, and women behind closed doors of the houses that lined the streets were tired from a week's work erasing the dirt from wealthy women's houses, playing nanny to wealthy women's kids, tending the aged long thrown away by their wealthy adult children.

I looked at the boy on the bike and thought of my own mother, my grandmother, and the grandmother before her, and answered, "No, they don't." I remembered my first training bras. Sewn inside the left flap of each was the name "Friedenburg." My bras, like my clothes, were throwaways from my grandmother's missus. "They hire black women to cook and clean and raise their kids. It allows them the freedom to come outside and burn their bras."

"I think my mother would like to meet you," was all he said by way of invitation, and I followed him off Hamilton Hill, past Union College, to a big house on Bradley Boulevard where beyond the front door was a library filled with books. And Audrey.

I'd read about her in the newspaper—the woman who dared reject an invitation to work for Governor Nelson Rockefeller. Tear gas from Attica still tasted filthy in her mouth. Rockefeller had held that gun. He could not now use the blackness of her face to wipe the smoke clear. "Mom, this is . . . what's your name?" he asked, and I realized I didn't know his either. My mother was going to kill me. One, I had ridden my bike to a forbidden part of town. And two, I'd followed a stranger to a strange house. But I didn't burn my $22 bra. That should count for something.

"Hello, Mrs. Harvey." I reached to shake her hand.

Her face was both warm and tough, crowned by a black afro adorned with one gray patch forming a star, right there above her widow's peak. "Who are you?" she asked abruptly, startling me, making me step back, looking to run.

He grinned. "She wouldn't burn her bra, Ma." There, all that was important had been said.

She smiled. "Good. Damn privileged white women." For hours we sat in that library, Audrey and I, talking about the rally, the solicitation of black women into this new feminist movement, and the bored Connecticut housewives who flocked to it. She talked, and as I listened, my eyes darted behind her to book jackets adorned with brown faces, bindings from which words like "black" and "power" leapt. I hadn't seen that before.

The afternoon passed easily, breezily in that library behind the front door. I left with the gift of James Baldwin's words in my hip pocket, *If Beale Street Could Talk*—the first book by a black author I ever owned. And all the way home, pedaling and sweating and running quick scenarios through my brain about what to tell my mother of my day, I kept envisioning Audrey's hair.

Mom wore a wig to hide an unruly pile of thin, feathery, dusty-brown naps persistent in their rebellion against curls, hot combs, and assortments of pomades. My hair was dark, what nylon wearers would call off-black, coarse, and fat. Biweekly I took it to O'Dell's for washing, drying, conditioning, hot combing, and curl. I hated it. I hated the burns on my ears and neck resulting from three hours of jerks and wiggles in the black plastic chair. I hated the smell of burning hair, that sweet, sickening smell of strands caught up in the comb placed on the blistering black iron skillet, and wondered if burning flesh smelled the same. That mixture of oil and heat, hair and spray that presented prettiness and culture was to me a thief that stole whole chunks of Saturday. For after a morning of primping and pain, play was forbidden, else the smooth false curls mix with nature's sweat and turn my hair back to its natural coarse naps at my roots and neck and the edges around my face. Why couldn't I just wear a wig?

"It's almost time for dinner. Wash your hands," was all Mom said, and I relaxed, sensing that trouble wasn't in the air. So I confessed.

"Mom, guess who I met today?"

"Who?" she asked.

"Audrey Harvey, the woman in the newspaper."

"Where? Did you meet her grandmother, too? Did I ever tell you about the time her grandmother kissed Nixon?" Before I could answer, between shuffling pots and plates and glasses, she told me how Ms. Jesselyne Payne kissed the president and enraged local blacks who thought that everyone of our hue ought to be Democrat or else shut up and be invisible. Mom, a Democrat too, was married to a Republican and couldn't quite grasp the hoopla. But hoopla there was, and Mom reminded me that if I was going to go against the grain, I better make sure I had thick skin.

"Can I visit again, Mom, Audrey, I mean?"

"I don't know her. But I know of her. Sure. You can visit again. If she asks." At last, I had a friend.

Identity and friendship, isolation and otherness, these were the makings of childhood, a private and burdensome struggle for a grade-school girl.

The evening before my departure to college in the bicentennial summer of independence, I called my cousin Myrtle, a jackleg hairstylist. She sat in a kitchen chair while I sat pensive on the floor between her legs, my back to her. Scissors in hand and electric clippers on the table, she cut and shaved my head near bald so that all there was to see was my face—big brown eyes, ragged eyebrows, high chubby cheeks, a mouth too small for my teeth—and the shadow of yesterday's hair. A million naps kinked around puffs of air, holding no weight at all, and fell around me onto my shoulders and her feet, to the cool tile floor. When she handed me the mirror to inspect what could not be undone, I brushed my hand against the soft bristles that covered my head, felt the boniness of my fingers slide across my scalp, smiled, and whispered, "Here I am."

In Which I Wade

Judith Chalmer

Sleep late and sleep long. Try it. See if it helps you. The small bows on the pillowcase, the smooth film of sweat on your face, that smell, the one deep inside warm hair, the hair of your mother, all will help you. Suicide and Spinoza, that sock stuck in your cousin's mouth the day he was dragged from his parents? Death, ever present? Sleep, I told you. Forget. That is the way I managed my childhood. Sleep. But not always. Some days I got on my bike and rode around. Some days I listened. In my forties, I began to talk. Here is a story I tell myself. If you need to, sleep through it. Try. If sleep doesn't help, you'll see something, a sign, perhaps hands that shake like a chain-metal gate. If sleep doesn't help, you can get up, move in closer. Go ahead, talk.

On an unsettled day in a city whose neighborhoods were as segregated in 1959 as the separate courses of a TV dinner, I forsook my mother's home and traveled on foot to a nearby vacant lot. My plan was to pole through the mud that stretched deep and unsupervised near the newly bricked school around the corner.

The lot was littered that early spring with sawed-off joists and the unused angles of plywood tossed to the reeds and forgotten by construction workers bent into the slush, hurrying home before Lake Erie dropped its slop pail of snow. That breezy spring day, on a time between Passover, when the Jews ran from Egypt, and Shavuous, when we dragged into Sinai, I went out, my destiny limited only by the reliability of my sneakers. I was eight and told to stay on the block, within unmarked but highly patrolled borders. In time, something less than forty years, bent stick splutting in and out of the mud, both feet braced on a triangle of ripped plywood, I reached a spit of dryish-looking land. Spying a cast-off dowel that looked useful for a makeshift tent, I stepped off my raft and stuck my foot in mud so deep I almost couldn't get out.

As far as I know, my mother died an old woman without knowing anything about my misstep and subsequent offense that day. Although we spoke deeply, self-appointed chaperones of the ungovernable century, and grateful for the few years of peace between us at last, we never, even once, spoke about the confusion of race and class that surrounded us as citizens, Jewish mother and daughter in North Buffalo, New York, United States. We never spoke of the differences in our relationships with the two black women who worked in our house during the years I was a child. I wouldn't have told her of the argument that followed my fall in the mud. It was impossible for me to piece together from the swirl of admiration and shame I held for my mother, for the Jewish people, for the America to which my parents and grandparents had come, even a temporary raft on which to pull out of, much less repair, the injustice in which I knew, even then, though I couldn't define it, we floundered, we fought, we held hands, we waded.

It was that summer when I was eight that my mother sat at my bed, her hand on my forehead, remembering her own childhood, her mother's hands that long-ago year when my mother herself was eight. As the headlights of the busy street traveled like a spaceship up the wallpaper in my room, my mother would describe the slow steps, hand in hand with her own mother up the steep hill, up out of the hot immigrant slum to the better neighborhood of Newark. Her mother, ever mindful of polio, wouldn't risk ice cream from the street vendors who called up from beneath the window of the flat where they lived over my grandfather's grocery, but would march in thick-seamed stockings to the drugstore, where ice-cream cones wore nurse's caps of folded waxed paper. It was that year, 1917, when my mother was eight, that her mother left one night for what my mother was told was a routine operation on a woman's parts, and died. Her father, old, a scholar and a grocer, weighed it all out and concluded, "I'm not really your father. I'm too old." My mother was put into foster care. Go to sleep now.

Go to sleep for forty years. The century has run down, all the way down my mother's hill. She was fifty years old when she told me that story, eighty-three when she died. I'm trying to weigh it all out: the mud; the challah; the streetlights; the smell of my mother's hair; brassy light from the samovar she kept polished, the one that was her father's; the Jewish America in which I was raised by my mother and two black maids. Leave it for another time, a few years, a decade. At eighteen, maybe, ask out loud and not of my mother, the night question, this business of fathers: Am I the child of a collaborator, a German Jew who got out early when no other Jew did, away from the Nazis? After a while it had been embarrassing to keep asking, "Ma, what was the name of that concentration camp again, where Daddy was?" Give me a few children of my own, my husband's non-German last name before I look for an answer. Give me more and more decades to find out that survival is attained by neither virtue nor sin, most often, but by luck. Send me back, to stand on the gravel-covered ground where my father labored in striped pajamas at Dachau, before I figure out we deserve to live not because of innocence, but because in ordinary ways, we're just human.

Jews are different. My mother's stories made that clear. Some better than others. It was my mother's family, for instance, that was in love with Pushkin, her older brother who read aloud to her, her father who'd closed his eyes for the last time in his bed, the book spread open on his chest, Spinoza. Never mind the daily onions, the beans and lettuce downstairs in the store. It was her father who dressed for dinner and retired to study, radiant and imposing, papers scattered on the floor. And so it was her family who balked later at the crass fiancé who'd just arrived in America via Dachau, with his German-Jewish arrogance, his childhood among Polish servants, his hands dirty with assimilationist money. The distrust between German and Russian Jews was something I'd grown up with. Did I ever hear about differences among black people? There was only one story I ever heard: universal poverty, unlettered ignorance, a solemn solidarity. A black middle class, a history of rhetoric or letters? In Buffalo? Anywhere? Never heard of it.

Lessons my mother taught me, some of which I learned: Don't be a burden. Don't ever go back. Take along your old father. If you're my mother, leave boarding-house foster care, sell stockings and handkerchiefs in order to get an apartment of your own where you can install the old father. Take the gas pipe, again if necessary, out of the old father's mouth.

I was ten when my mother told me about suicide. Again she sat on my bed, her wide-ribbed back rocking like a rowboat. After the death of the old father, my mother married glamour, a man who memorized opera verses. Wealth. Railroad wealth. No, he was Jewish. It wasn't the railroad owner's wealth. It was lawyers-to-the-railroad, Pullman Company, wealth. There were cruises to London, a trousseau of monograms. There were speakeasies and long, luxurious smokes. It was the Village in the '20s. There was wife swapping. And lies. Unbearable, dangerous, never-spoken-by-my-mother, financial lies. Soon we'll get to the suicide. My mother rows, next to me in the bed, our small white boat. The number 9 bus stops at the corner of Parkside and Starin. Reezey, after caring for my sister and me all day, steps up from the cobbled bus stop. Transfer ticket, please. I know nothing about her family's choices, her dead husband, whether or not he had life insurance, her parents, a single day at her school, or in church. Back to bed, the sheets for sails, my mother rowing. My mother takes me to the '30s. Depression. Prohibition. My mother walks the Jersey shore, considering. "I would have gotten more support for suicide than for divorce." My heart swells, is bigger than the bed. She lived. My mother chose. She's next to me in my bed. She got no alimony; she considered herself lucky just to get out.

For my mother, as for many women, education rather than marriage was the option that compared best to suicide. I don't know how she paid for it, probably reluctantly accepting help from extended family, but I do know she took an M.S.W. and went to work for the Red Cross in Tampa, Florida. It was

World War II, and there, in Tampa, caring for shell-shocked soldiers, she met and married my father, also a soldier, a social-worker soldier in the U.S. Army. There he is, my father, Mr. Uniform. Let's salute. I have, of course, no actual memory of him. I'll compile a dossier for him. *Geboren:* 1906, Aschaffenburg, Germany. Profession: Lawyer, not allowed to practice by Nuremberg decree. Arrested, November 10, 1938, the morning after Krystallnacht. Sent directly to Dachau. Gets out. Gets out. Was it only a few weeks? He barely suffered, I whisper, the bile of the "real" survivors pooling in my heart. January 1939, he leaves Germany for good. Maybe not for good. I have a photo of him, my parents' wedding photo. I crawl up to the attic to look at it. My father in uniform. My father, who saved himself, left the others behind, like babies, defenseless. Put away the photo album. Put it back in the cupboard. It's better to sleep.

My mother had one baby, a boy named Mark, while my father was somewhere unknown. Somewhere, again, back in Germany. Joining the army was a way to get U.S. citizenship quickly, and because he spoke German fluently, army intelligence sent him, of course, you know where. The baby lived about two weeks. On May 8, 1945, the army gave my father compassionate leave, but news of the baby's death did not reach him; his fond letters home, anticipating small fingers curled all at once around just one of his own, continued for weeks while my mother battled grief and pneumonia after the baby's death. Meanwhile, my father found his sister, found the little boy, the one she let go with a sock in his mouth so he wouldn't cry when a stranger took him to hiding. They are newly reunited with his mother, my grandmother, in turn freshly returned from her winter in Westerbork concentration camp. They bristle with Germanic sounds. Like chainlink fences with metallic voices, they shake.

When my father returned, my mother learned an important lesson: Never work in the same agency as your husband. It's not good for a marriage, competition from a wife. Remember that, Judelein. But there's good news. It's a job for my father, a new start in Buffalo, director of Jewish Family Services. It's enough money to bring over all the surviving family, one by one. My mother never did tell him of her illness, of spirit and body, after their baby's death. "After what he'd been through, I didn't feel entitled." Decades later, a social worker who had worked at Jewish Family Services under my father's supervision told me she'd had no idea he had been a refugee himself. My sister was born in 1947, then I in 1951. Now we're back where we started. Reezey is coming in again, by the back door. I did not know what her grandparents, her parents escaped, left behind. She hangs her coat in the back hall. Our dog, Midnight, piddles delight on top of her shoes.

When my father died, my mother decided to stay in Buffalo, out of biting range from the family. The total amount of life insurance money she collected went to buy the house down whose back basement stairs I threw my aforementioned muddy sneakers on that fine spring day when I went out to probe the mud surrounding the new American synagogue. My mother had, thank heavens, her profession and could hire Reezey to watch her two children and do light housework while she was gone. Am I collecting these credentials of suffering to justify my mother's benefiting at last from a well-earned system of injustice? They are stories, each with a name: Rosie the Orphan. Rosie the Daring Young Flapper. Rose the Widow. Professor Ma. With these names I know her. Through them I learned to be fierce, to withstand certain sorrow. They are stories within stories, stories overlapping other stories, stories with some chance, some choice. Without them, without such stories, such names, particular hands on particular heads, I did not know the women who, with families likewise buffeted about by world powers and fateful deaths, boarded buses every day without tenure, without health insurance, and with a full sink of dishes at home, to care for me, to listen and joke with my mother.

What kept me from those stories? Why did it never occur to me to ask? Were there trains and laws and accents that sharpened Reezey's or Vesta's dreams? Why couldn't I imagine, in even the broadest of terms, two different cultures, that of Vesta's Southern, rural family and Reezey's of the industrial North? Were there other children, nieces, nephews, in their lives? What photos hung in their parlors? Whose were the mouths, what chewed? Who and in what way were swallowed? If, when my mother needed to work and raise young kids in Buffalo, it was underpaid personal service provided by black women that became the thought, the possibility, the answer, what else would have constituted a good choice? What education shaped the hopes of my mother, Reezey, and Vesta? What, to them, and through them to me, was the cost? What choices are there, for me, now? I can, in keeping with my mother, who in the late 1930s organized social workers into a union, dedicate myself to good working conditions for domestic workers: defined hours, sick pay, insurance, fees commensurate with clinicians for emotional services provided. What if I don't like the excessive consumption that makes personal services relevant for physically able adults? Shall I, in keeping with my Marxist grandfather, determine that domestic work is a form of capitalist exploitation? What is a Jewish response to women who apply, seek out, such jobs? What is a Jewish response to women who provide them? With what accusation do I confront my mother, when I view our lives together, knowing the actions we took, the words we spoke were part of a racist structure within which we were somewhat less autonomous than I once imagined? How do I help dismantle what's before me when I must also dismantle what I stand on, all that lies behind? Remember the viaduct over Starin Avenue, between

Taunton and St. Lawrence? Say anything about my mother and I'll take you there and beat the shit out of you, I swear it.

I have almost nothing to say about Reezey. She carried me, changed my diapers, fed me. She was neither warm and enveloping nor punishing. When she wasn't busy, she sat on a step stool in the kitchen. Like my mother, she was old to be taking care of children. She'd lost a husband in World War II. She held the line against my mother's bitter lament, refusing to make my mother tea, listen to her day, or do heavy housework. I think now about the support she might have had at home, at church, for holding that line. I look back and wonder in which direction over it her care for me pulled her.

Reezey and my mother kept a clean distance pulled tight between them. And the house was sheathed in gray. My mother worried, didn't know how to manage on one woman's salary. She came home, cooked a careful supper, lifted herself up the stairs to her room, groaned out of her girdle, put her head down . . . gray hair, grayer nights. Sometimes now, I imagine my mother at the age I am. I think of her with a four-year-old and an eight-year-old at forty-six, in the middle of the night, I'm sick, and it's the 1950s, when single mothering, at least in our neighborhood, wasn't even a term. Laugh, Ma. Laugh. Look over here, in the doorway, it's me, the monster's daughter. Watch me walk like a toad. Ma. What's the matter?

I was five when my mother married Morris and we were suddenly back in the money. The world cracked open, and out of that crack poured color and sparkle, heat, blond furniture, a real hi-fi, lamb chops, my mother glowing orchard bright. I had a new big sister, suddenly, peacock bright. I was six when Morris died. One morning, playing cards with my sister, I watched him walk down the hall, along the stairs on one side, past the door to the kitchen on the other, brush past the coats hanging on their metal stand at the end of the hallway, turn sharp left into the little square bathroom under the stairs, fall back out, get up, and fall down again, like a doll, like a punching bag. Get up, Daddy. I'm punching you, now you bounce back. Get it? You get back up. That's two, so far, two fathers who have died within a year of contact with me.

Reezey was there the year my stepfather burst in like a bright feathered arrow and shot back out. Perhaps she put me to sleep. I don't know. I don't remember. Whoever put me to sleep did it well. It was a thorough job. What I know is that out of that sleep I forged the sense of myself that was to last through my thirties: murderer, monster's daughter. I reasoned it out: My own father died the year I was born. It was a bad thing to do. If he was the monster I feared he was, then he'd turned Nazi while in Dachau in order to use his law degree to get the law to let him out. In that case, he collaborated with the Nazis and that was the source for me, of breath, existence, life. If he was, as my mother told me, kind, brilliant, and honest, well then, he'd died because he didn't want to be near me, I being for sure not kind, brilliant, or honest. I, the murderer myself of two fathers.

My mother was, meanwhile, clawing her way back into life. She did it with the help of Vesta, whom she hired to do heavy housework on weekends. My mother clung to Vesta, who was, like Reezey, black, and considered her both confidante and helpmate. Vesta took care of my sister and me as well. Vesta said I scared her with my temper. In turn, I hated Vesta. My mother, for all her grief, was moving fast in those days, staking out territory at the university where she worked. She was a crossover, a maverick social worker in the psychology department. There were cocktail parties at which Vesta served in the starched whites she always wore to work. There was art and social policy at the dinner table. My mother's eyes were bright as sheriff's badges. At five foot two, a matzoh-ball shape from shoulder to soft hip, she took up more social space than her body occupied, and the space, once taken, was not allowed to remain soft but was hard. She was associate professor, then director of the teaching clinic, the very first M.S.W. to be made full professor. This was on the strength of her ability to look you in the eye, to talk. She never published. It was a first, at that school, for a woman or for a man. My mother took pride in being the first person on the block to invite to our house the first black professor who moved into our neighborhood. This was about the time my friends' parents began buying houses in the suburbs. Memberships at private swimming clubs became awfully popular. My mother must have carried a fair amount of fury in her arms when she opened the front door, standing to the side as if she were pulling the heavy curtains open on a stage, to welcome them. I'm sure she took pleasure in making her point to the other white neighbors, although as I recall only blank windows looked on. And there was Reezey every day through the back door, Vesta on weekends.

My mother was undone with Vesta, charmed and gracious. Sometimes there was no way to avoid them together. What got to me was the laughter. My mother put on a fake Southern accent and called Vesta "honey chile." I think there were magnolias in the conversation, and food cooked so well it could only have been made by people who know it to be precious. I know there were poultices and compresses, a million things for tears. There were hot, dusty roads Vesta traveled back on once a year. My mother called Vesta's stories of her mother "folktales." My mother called her own memories "what happened." I lurked at the door and watched Vesta. She kept her shoulders humped, her head down, so that though she was taller than the professor, she was always looking up. Her lips curled up when she laughed and her teeth showed all the way up to the gums. What were they doing? I whaled on my older sister, threw dolls and screeched if she got near me. I slammed the door on her head. Vesta didn't like to baby-sit me. My stepsister came home from college with her boyfriend from the South. There was more laughter, some strange ability to talk to someone who turned herself into a chimpanzee in your presence, more stories and jokes, Vesta humping her shoulders. I don't know where I am, but wherever it is, I want out. I think, What Vesta is doing, turning herself into a monkey, is wrong, ugly wrong. Doesn't each of us, I think, have in that moment complete and independent freedom of choice? Mine? Go to sleep. In their presence, refuse to speak. What did you say?

When I was twelve and my older sister sixteen, my mother called me to the kitchen. Reezey sat on her chair under the clock, hair in a bun, solid in her middle age as my mother. My mother used the voice she used to explain to me what will happen at a funeral. Reezey won't be here much longer. She won't always be coming back. I'm letting her go. Okay, can I go now? Don't you want to kiss her? I don't care. I'm going to sleep. Wake me up a few decades later. Did I say I knew nothing of Reezey? There is one thing I remember about Reezey. As she sat on the step stool under the clock in the kitchen, she could hear me playing about. Each time I burped, she would prompt me, "What did you say?" until I knew to say "Excuse me" myself. As she sat on the step stool under the clock in the kitchen, I could hear her breathing. I could hear her every burp. And when I prompted her, "What did you say?" she laughed the laugh of a teacher, the teacher who delights in what the child decides to carry on.

Excuse me. There's one thing more. Reezey said all she wanted, someday, all she asked of me as an adult someday, was to be invited to my wedding. When it came to pass, someone said, "Reezey and Vesta can serve." I, to whom Reezey had told her request, was quiet. And Reezey refused. She came to my wedding, and sat. Vesta served. Reezey refused to serve. Some years later, my mother told me on the phone she'd forgotten to mention that a few weeks earlier Reezey had died. I turned red, but was silent. I don't know if my mother's resentment of Reezey or my own deadened, half-asleep response to leavings, to betrayal, to death, kept me quiet. I certainly hadn't kept in touch with her. I'm not sure which of us, during my mother's phone call, Reezey or I, was the more alive. What words would she say today, now that I'm old enough to ask? What words now can I find to remember, respect the line Reezey held? What and whose words will retrieve the anger she must have felt, but could not speak to us at the time? Face in the mirror: "What did you say?"

I do know that when I was eight years old, returning from a vacant lot with freedom all over my pants, freedom in my hair, my eyes, I felt entitled to throw my sneakers down the basement stairs. They were all but ripped, dirty. I didn't want them. The next weekend they appeared, clean, in my room. I didn't ask anyone to clean them. Again, I threw them away. And I remember Vesta charging upstairs the next day, my clean sneakers in her hands. I remember her hands, shaking like a metal fence, her voice choked, charred as if by ashes, her accusation: "I worked all day to clean those shoes, and you think you can just throw them away."

I hated her for that. I hated Vesta. I was not too young to understand her rage. I said nothing to her, though my face grew very red. I never asked her to clean them, I said. It wasn't my idea to have her there. I wouldn't have made the basement her workstation. I was better than that. What did you say?

I say, my life now and forever includes Vesta's workstation and everything I contributed to it. I say, it's taken me a long time to realize I can't throw away the pain, the moral compromise of that workstation, that work system, just because I don't like it. It's taken me a long time to say, silence will neither exonerate nor protect me.

That wasn't the only time I considered myself trapped by my mother, and by Vesta. By the time I was college age, my mother was sixty years old. Anxiety was beginning to overpower her pride at work. Neither my sister, recently eloped, nor I would talk to her. Once my mother made a test of me, for days holding speech at bay, waiting to see if I would speak first, then finally, in exasperation, crying, "How long can a person live in the same house and not say something?" She, by then, had grown used to Vesta's availability for "field work," (under)paid emotional services, and took Vesta as companion on the car trip to Michigan, where I would be mercifully ensconced at college, five hours from home. There were several trips up the dormitory stairs from the car. By the time I finished carrying bags to my room, Vesta had made my bed in her starched whites, hospital corners and all. It would have been my first act of independence there, to make my own bed. It was done by our maid. It was 1969. I looked at Vesta and at my mother, so insistent on my separation, my autonomy from their choices, their lives. So willfully ignoring the something far bigger than personal blame, far more urgent to acknowledge, to answer, to claim. I wanted only to banish the visible pain that made knowledge of my complicity inevitable. My hands were shaking, my face red. I turned away.

It's a new century, more than a decade since my mother's death. I never did keep track of the dates Reezey, first, then Vesta died. I can say nothing of their funerals, nothing of their homes, nothing of their lives. I can say it took me almost a quarter of a century to move near again to my mother, to tell her this, this is my life, without fear I'd be swallowed. I find myself now, at my son's bar mitzvah, at work, camping with friends under the stars, telling stories about her, thinking how she might have done some small thing I now must do. I know her, if not completely, then at least in many stories, her hair changing to pepper and salt, sea-mist gray, her names on my lips tasting of plum cake and ashes.

I think about my silence in the presence of two women I was too arrogant to thank, too selfish to ask, too young to imagine in their human forms of ambiguity. I think about having aimed my anger, my understanding that I was compromised, at the nearest adults. I think about the imagery that in 1959 circled the house: deepest, darkest Africa . . . jungles where people lived with/like the beasts . . . cartoon illustrations of Little Black Sambo, *Amos 'n' Andy* on the radio, Raahhchester and the Boss. I think of having thought Vesta's open mouth, her shoulders, like those of a chimpanzee. I think about how those images came in, into me in my mother's house, and I want to know, through which windows? I think about the paralysis I felt but could not name, having been born into a system where racism grew for me, in me, not nearly so much out of what I might have done, as out of what history I dared not know. I am beginning to see there is no choice for me now but to act, every day and with every word, within the terms of race and class I've inherited, even while striving to change, to undermine them. There is no turning away, no neutrality in silence. I cling to the boards and the words of my history as an American Jewish woman, those rafts that propel me to question. Hip deep in America, I continue this way, bearing history's cargo, to wade.

A Child's Christmas in Revere

Patricia Goodwin

Revere, 196_

Ma stood at the kitchen window, smoking one Tareyton after another, peering out the night window that blinked with Christmas lights like a pinball machine. Whimpering and clawing at her legs was her little terrier, Tareyton, named after her cigarette, and the commercial for the cigarette where all the Tareyton smokers have one black eye, just like the terrier.

"Jesus!" Ma growled through her teeth, clamped down on the cigarette as she bent down to pick up the wiggly little rat. "She's killing me! My legs!"

Ma resumed her gaze out the window, sending bullets of radar into the car lights rushing toward her.

"Christ Almighty, where the hell is he?"

I didn't pay too much attention to her. I was running into the kitchen to get my fiftieth low-calorie snack of the evening, an apple, maybe, or a piece of cheese, sliced clandestinely from the large chunk in the refrigerator, getting smaller, a tiny mouse nibbling it away.

I ran back to my all-consuming life in the living room, the details of which I have forgotten, though not completely. And I also haven't forgotten how seriously I took those fantasies and fables to heart. Maybe it was *The Addams Family*—after all, Ma called me Morticia because of my long hair; maybe *Robin Hood,* to whom I played Maid Marian in my mind; maybe *Walt Disney's Wonderful World of Color,* which we got in wonderful black and white. Jakey and I used to argue about what the colors might be. If you knew one, like Santa's red suit, for instance, you could almost guess what the others might be. Always, I was sure I was right; it's a lost skill, or maybe, I was always wrong.

How deeply we lost ourselves in the darkness and the blue light flickering. It erased the floor, the ceiling, the walls, and everyone around me. Only TV Land existed.

That night I was intent on getting back to whatever drama was playing itself out on the screen, but as I rushed past her, Ma's torment pulled at my careless mind and body. I didn't have any idea how much she needed Daddy to set up the Christmas presents under the tree, that Christmas might not happen without him. I was old enough to question the existence of Santa Claus, and young enough to forget I questioned it.

Besides, she was always waiting for him, always standing right there at that window, smoking, begging the horizon to produce his car lovingly zooming toward her. I'll never wait for a man! I vowed as I ran by her, convinced she was an idiot; yet, half my heart remained with her, standing at that window, hugging her with that squirmy, maggoty dog.

Deep in TV Land, once more floating in the virtual world, I can still hear the front door open, with its peculiar *ssquee-runch!* It stuck in damp and swollen weather.

"There he is!" Ma's heart sighed audibly, while her dog burst into the frenzied howling of a terrier.

Daddy's cheerful, proud-of-himself face came in, beaming full, catching the streetlight from outside. But what was that with him? Against the black night behind Daddy's shoulders was a black shape following him, then eyes, shiny bits of white, staring eyes. Eyes, flipping from side to side. Tall eyes at first, then short eyes, flipping even faster, two little pairs of them.

Colored people!

What were colored people doing in our house?

Terrified little children, a boy and a girl, about four and five years old, standing close to their mother, tall, pretty, eyes cautious, staring. Next to her a colored man, taller than Daddy, angry, chin set hard, eyes furious as a man in chains.

The children inched backward into their mother, her eyes round and determined. She held her kids by their shoulders as they shivered with fear, then gently, pushed them forward; patient, she was. Slowly, the children came into the living room, where three white kids sat gape-mouthed and cross-legged on the floor. The man, angry as hell, and Daddy, a beacon of hospitality, stood in the doorway. Daddy introduced his kids.

He got our names right, but not our ages, not that anyone cared. I didn't know then how drunk he was, only that he was bringing in colored people.

Ma ran in from the kitchen. Now that I'm older, I can see her in my mind stubbing out her cigarette, tossing her barking, clawing dog into the pantry and quickly shutting the door, getting her brain in order: My husband has brought colored people home with him, there are colored people in my house—what to do?

Rush to the door and welcome them.

"Their car broke down on the parkway," Daddy explained to Ma. "I said, 'It's Christmas Eve! Come home with me; don't stand out here in the cold, come home with me! The little lady will make us some coffee, get warm! Eh, we'll go back for the car later!' Make us some coffee, Rosie, will you?"

The two trembling kids were deposited with us in the dark living room, while the adults went into the kitchen. Kids were always just dumped with kids; adults went with adults.

It was Jakey who spoke to them. He was used to colored people, though I don't know how—maybe from the carnies on the beach, or it might have been from the track people, though neither of these groups seemed especially colored to me. The one other time I'd seen a colored person, I was about two. She was a little girl, and she was standing on the other side of a chainlink fence in Connecticut, where we were visiting my sister Marie's godmother, who was a lot nicer than mine and pretended to be my godmother also, only she wasn't pretending—she meant it. The second I saw the little colored girl dressed in a frilly pink dress, I busted out screaming. I thought she was a monster in a pretty little dress. The adults came running out of the house and laughed at me. "Oh, Gloria! Don't be silly! It's just a little girl, see!" But I was terrified. The little girl just stared at me; she nibbled on her finger. Maybe she was wondering what the heck I was, maybe some kind of screaming alien, with a big mouth, an enormously high forehead, feathery yellow tufts, and bulging green eyes.

"You ever watch this show?" Jakey asked the little boy.

He nodded vigorously. All five of us kids returned to TV Land and floated together. We didn't say another word to each other.

Which was why we could hear every word from the kitchen.

Daddy's voice boomed, large and generous.

"We're *all equal! All equal!!* I've always said, 'We're all equal!' In the eyes of the law and the eyes of God! You want another beer?"

A quiet answer, angry.

"Go on! There's more where that came from. Some of my best friends in the Merchant Marines! There was Joseph—we called him Black Ben because he wore those little half-glasses like Ben Franklin, you know; and Cookie—what was his name, what a guy! Give you the shirt off his back, that guy! By God, you're all equal out on the sea! You can't fool Mother Nature, you know! She'll drown a white man quick as a colored any day, she doesn't know the difference!"

"She doesn't know the difference." His eyes going blank over a long sip of beer. His upper lip curled in a funny way over the lip of the glass because he didn't have all his teeth anymore. His lip curled and I felt it curl, in my tummy, where I can still feel the horrid sensation of his lip.

I could see him. I was there, in the kitchen. I must have ventured into the adult world.

"Ah!" He swallowed a whiskey chaser. "Don't worry about the car, now! It's too cold to worry. Don't worry!"

"We're all equal." Daddy's eyes, bloodshot and liquid. He wiped a tear.

The women drank coffee.

"That Martin Luther King, and Jack Kennedy—they had the right idea, by God! Damn shame, it's all our shame, by God."

On the edge of their seats, the women quietly drank coffee. They exchanged a few, soft words.

I remember the fierce jaw of the man. Maybe he didn't like a little blonde girl staring at him. Maybe he didn't like Daddy.

I wondered if he wanted to be helped. It was his family's Christmas Eve, too. Maybe he didn't want us in his Christmas. As if in conspiracy with the colored man, Daddy took out his oily wallet and from the secret black folds, he pulled an old piece of folded newspaper. He moved carefully, as though the yellowed, soiled paper were an archeological treasure, the black oil of a hundred machines caught in its dry creases, his thick, blackened fingers made suddenly graceful, as they must have been handling the infinitesimal body parts of the gargantuan machines he fixed every day. How much blood had Daddy poured from his veins into those machines? How much of his flesh had been chewed by the oily black teeth of gears? How many volts of electricity vibrated through his tendons and bones? Careful, as though unfolding a great secret, he spread the newspaper, which turned out to be a photo of a machine as big as a room. In front of this machine stood Daddy, in his work uniform, the young Daddy, who looked so very much like Alan Ladd with the love curl curling, and another man, in a dark suit. The man in the suit had his arm tightly around Daddy. Both men were grinning like devils.

Daddy pointed his smallest fingernail at his own tiny head in the picture. "That's me," he said. "Don't tell me I don't know what it's like to be colored."

The man's jaw twitched ever so slightly. Daddy handed him the photo. In his big, black hands, carved brown and pale as coffee with cream on the palms, in his hands, the photo looked small. It looked almost white.

"I invented that machine," Daddy explained. "Ever hear of the shrink-wrap machine?"

The man's head rose quickly. He knew.

"I had to find a way to heat the wrap—that was the problem, you know—I had to find a way to heat the wrap without heating the food underneath." Daddy grinned the same devilish grin he'd had in the photograph. "How do you think I did that?"

"I did it! I solved it!"

And Daddy told the man how he'd finally perfected the shrink-wrap machine. But I didn't understand a word, because I didn't care anything about shrink-wrap at that time. I cared more for the television I was missing, or the food I decided to get, I don't remember which it was. I remain, today, with only the astonishment of how close I once came to waking up a princess.

"And who do you think got the credit? Whose name is on that machine now? Who got the patent? Who got rich?"

I turned just in time to see that huge, black finger point to the employer's now-sinister, smiling face.

"He did." The only words I heard him speak, with a strange, thick drawl.

"You're right! Goddamn it! You're right! The man who paid for it! That's who! Tell me I don't know what it's like to be colored!"

The man left with Daddy to go out into the freezing winter night to the highway, where Daddy would fix his abandoned car with a flashlight and his toolbox. The women remained in the kitchen, nearly silent, drinking coffee. We kids watched a lot of TV that night, until Daddy and the man returned and the parents ushered their children out. As they passed in front of the TV, TV Land shifted from a vital, three-dimensional reality to flat shapes with talking mouths. As the man passed, his jaw was just as hard-set and cold as it had been when he entered, as hard and cold as the frozen road under Daddy's back as he'd lain under the car like Michelangelo under the ceiling of the Sistine Chapel. I wanted to shout from the place I was, in the blue dark of TV Land, shout to the man, "He means it! You don't know him! Just because he's drunk doesn't mean he doesn't mean it!" But it wouldn't have been enough. Being drunk and sincere wasn't enough.

Daddy missed Christmas that year. He slept through it.

In the diluted gray morning, Ma, who'd tried for hours to wake him and couldn't, phoned her saintly brothers, Uncle Salvi and Uncle Sonny, to come and set up Christmas for us. They put my new bike together and brought the games and other boxes over from Grandma's, where they'd been hidden. The bike was from Uncle Vickie, who got it "off a truck," and the games were from Uncle Salvi, who was rich. Uncle Sonny was too young to be able to buy nice presents. Uncle Vickie also gave me two plastic dresses like they wore on *Hullabaloo,* only with the price tags still on them.

Daddy woke up the day after and held his sick head in his hands and sipped a Bloody Mary in that funny way with his upper lip suspended over the rim of the glass.

"A hair of the dog that bit me," he usually said, but not this time.

This time, Daddy vowed never to abuse drink again, because then he'd have to give it up, and "God forbid."

The Last Safe Place

Toiya Kristen Finley

8.

I've waited three hours.

I handed out four invitations last week. Swept and polished and vacuumed my room clean until there was no dust. A room that stays cluttered months on end even when my mother and grandmother offer bonuses to my allowance. It's clean now, though, because my friends are going to spend my birthday weekend with my small family.

I've waited four hours.

Staring at the black-and-white TV my grandmother gave me, the TV I plan for my friends and I to watch late at night while we stay up and pretend we're big girls. I make trips up and down the stairs, peek outside the front door and check the street for my friends' parents' cars. The first hour, when I asked my mother if she thought they were lost, she said she didn't know. Now she looks at me to tell me she knows they were never lost, they were never coming.

I've waited until it doesn't matter anymore.

Even though my four friends aren't coming, I'm still staring at the black-and-white TV wondering what it would have been like if we were all here in my room now. I've been to their houses many times—it doesn't make sense that they can't come to mine, that their parents won't let them.

"You can go to their houses, but they can't come to yours," my mother says.

Maybe their parents think this is the bad part of town. If this were a weekend I was staying with my father, I could see why they wouldn't want their daughters with me. The boy from across the street might come over to play video games, and his parents might come to get him. They sell cocaine out of their house. Cocaine and lots of other things. The two boys next door sell bootlegs out of a crooked man's car. The women fuss, and the men spend all night playing cards because they live their days empty.

But this is not my father's neighborhood. This is my grandmother's, and everyone is middle class here. Some are barely middle class, but we are all still middle class. There're no gunfights in the middle of the street. No door-to-door robberies. The kids all plan to go to college, and the grown-ups don't complain about their jobs because they pay well.

Monday morning, I'll get the excuses from my four friends. They'll be better than "I couldn't come just because I couldn't come." And I'll believe them. At school, we can laugh it off. At school, we always laugh off the world of grownups, although the grownups made the school for us. Made it a few years after other grownups put up all-white private schools in response to integration. But they wear uniforms, and their mascots are rebels, and there are hardly any non-white students. They go to Christian schools, Christian like me, but I don't understand the brand they teach.

Here, we don't wear uniforms. We're encouraged to be as individual as we care to. We sing Christmas and Hanukkah songs at the winter music concert and "We Shall Overcome" and the Black National Anthem during Black History Month. We learn about Diwali and Kwanza and Ramadan. Rabbis visit and give us plastic dreidels. My Jewish and Christian and Muslim friends all get along, even though the TV and, sometimes, their parents say they cannot. This is the only place I know to find Hindus, and they're my friends, too. Some of my friends came from Japan and Italy, their accents thick, but we always manage a way to communicate. We're white and black and yellow and red and cinnamon and our hair is kinky and straight and curly and we're rich and not-so-rich, and nobody cares.

The grown-up world has nothing on us.

But now I'm at home and not at school, and I'm staring at the black-and-white TV wondering how I'm going to spend my weekend alone.

If only my four friends' parents knew this neighborhood was not like my father's. That there are good black parts to Nashville.

It's only a misunderstanding.

10.

We wait for our teacher to take us to drama class, my two close friends and I. One's family comes from the Middle East, from places too far away for me to imagine. The other has an important Nashville family. She's never come to my grandmother's house. They don't usually stand this close together, my two good friends, but they have me in common. One takes a look at the legs of the other, jumps back, and screws up her face. "Gross! You need to shave your legs. They're all hairy. They're *soooo* hairy."

I never noticed it on her legs before. Spinning around her shins and thighs as black and long and beautiful as the hair on her head. The hair on my legs never grows beyond stubble, and I would never think of putting a razor to my skin. I have never heard of such a thing, women putting a blade to their legs. My other friend has scabby thin lines all over her legs, ruined.

"You shave your legs?" I say. "*That's* gross. It's stupid."

"You're supposed to shave your legs."

"I've never heard of it," I say.

"But you're supposed to. Not shaving 'em's stupid. Nobody wants to look at that."

"Not everybody does," I say, but the other girl never says anything.

My mother isn't surprised to find out women shave their legs when I tell her. "White women *like* to shave their legs," she says. It's a ritual, an entrance into womanhood as mother and daughter fret over not cutting the skin. For me it's still disgusting and weird, but white people, I've been told, are weird in many ways.

So tomorrow we'll be back at school walking around with our hairy and shaved legs, knowing that this is the way we choose to live within our skin.

Today is only a misunderstanding.

14.

We're forced to wait here in the auditorium. There are microphones in front of the stage. Everything's been set up for us, but no one's ready to speak. The faculty has left us alone because they've always taught us to be independent. We are fourteen to eighteen years old. We can work this out ourselves.

I wonder, though, as I sit in this row, if that's really why they've left us alone. It wasn't that long ago when one of my teachers said nothing because she didn't know what to say, during one of those free-flowing discussions, one of those times when a tangent can lead to just about anything, can lead us so far off topic we wonder how we dared to wander so far astray.

So we were on black people and television when we were supposed to be reading Shakespeare in freshman English class. Now that there were a few black shows scattered across network television, there was no need for BET, some said. Black Entertainment Television, with its news shows and music, comedy and black sitcoms from other parts of the world. It was no longer important, they said. Not with *Martin* and *The Fresh Prince of Bel-Air.*

Me, I never really watched BET, but I knew faces like mine weren't on TV enough. I couldn't shut down the aggravation and anxiety that had built up within me. "We need our own shows," I said. The faces around the room were hard or blank and uninterested. No faces like mine. I was the only non-white student in the classroom.

"You *have* your own shows."

"Only a few comedies. We need more than that. We need stuff about us, that thinks the way we think."

"You *have* that."

"How do you know?" I said.

"BET is *racist,*" they said.

My white friends said nothing. My white teacher said nothing.

And, because I supported a racist network, that meant I was racist, too.

I hadn't intended to cry when I told my mother. But I sobbed loud and hard, the dirty label of racist trying to worm its way into my heart. Racists were bitter black women who gossiped about white whores stealing their men. Racists were blacks who admitted they hated white people but couldn't be racist because they didn't have political power, and the kids at church who treated me like an Oreo because of the school I attended. Racists wore pointy white hats or committed genocide somewhere on the other side of the world. Racism had no place at my school.

My mother called my teacher, demanded to know how we had all gone so far astray. My teacher didn't know what to do. Knew things were out of control. Didn't know how to stop it. She offered to let me say something before the class the next day. The first and last time I ever snapped at a teacher, and I rested in the satisfaction of getting away with it. My teacher stood in front of me with her mouth hanging open, knowing she could not respond. I wouldn't defend myself anymore. It was too late for explanations. The lines had already been crossed.

All of us gathered here in the auditorium—this has the same feeling as that day during freshman English with no teacher present who knows what to do, how to guide us. We're alone and forced to wait in the auditorium. Forced to settle "our" problems during what should have been a free period.

We stare at the microphones standing in front of the stage. We don't look at each other. My row, we all feel the same thing. Only girls sitting here, squished as close as we can get, as if our shared body heat could bring security. On one side of me, a close friend with the hair black and long and beautiful as the hair on her head waxed off of her legs. On the other, my half-Lebanese, half-Italian friend. We are freshmen, sophomores, juniors, and seniors, all on this row. Taiwanese, black, biracial, and Tamil. Even the two Thai sisters sit with us. With very little English, maybe they don't really know what's going on, but they're here with us.

We're here because someone defaced a copy of *Jet*. In the high school library, someone took a marker to an ad, drew comic-strip balloons from the mouths of the black man and woman. Made them talk about eating fried chicken and watermelon. It was difficult for our teachers to tell us. They couldn't get the culprit to confess. It was difficult for us to talk about it when our teachers first announced it during classes. It was hard for us even to believe it. We'd just had t-shirts printed for the high school—Unity Through Diversity, they said proudly on the front. They had a yin-yang symbol drawn in green and purple instead of white and black. A gifted black student designed it and drew students on the back pursuing science and art and literature and sports. This was the last safe place, where the worldviews outside need not apply.

Once the first one dares, a steady stream of students approaches the microphone. This was just one individual, they say, who doesn't represent the rest of us. This school has been good to us, they say. Some of them would know. They have been here since kindergarten. This school allows us to be ourselves, they say. There is so much diversity. They are shouting this.

They are all white.

None of us go up to the microphones. No non-white student will dare, although we have something to say. We have a lot to say, but we'll transfer it in the security of our body heat, in our anger, as we huddle closer together. Out of the corner of our eyes, we watch the other non-white students shake invisibly as they bite hard on their bottom lips.

What happened to the *Jet* has nothing to do with us, they say up at the mics. We are not racists. We believe in unity. This is one little incident that will not happen again. It's ridiculous we even have to be here. They seem to be saying all the right things, but they're still angry. Still shouting. They don't need us to come up and say anything. They can say it for us.

There's something rising up in us, here on this row. Echoes of things our parents have told us. Legends of conflicts. The painful looks I get from my mother and grandmother when they see me riding in the back of a white friend's car. Even when I've chosen to ride back there. Lessons given by the old folk in our communities—white people are sneaky, white people don't care, white people don't understand.

They scan the audience from behind the mics. In the classroom, it would be all right—but right now, they don't want to hear our hairy-legged points of view. We stare, too, stare them straight in the eyes, take back the invitations to our houses. Right now, they are not welcome . . . if they ever were.

Some upperclassman I don't know and would never know comes up to the microphone. He's infuriated. He shouts. He screams. It's ridiculous, he says, that we even have to be here, forced into this auditorium. This is a waste of our time. On this we can all agree. He yells, one last time, that racism has no place here. It is not here. Then he leaves, the sound of his footsteps echoing around us. He throws the middle doors open. They crash behind him, rattling the rest of us silent.

In the next few weeks, the faculty will admit they should never have left us alone. We will begin reading more literature on other cultures. We'll take trips to see culturally appropriate movies. Our principal will start a support group for all of the black students—whether we want support or not.

Tomorrow, we will pretend this incident never happened. We'll go back to proudly wearing our Unity Through Diversity shirts.

Right now, though, we sit here until someone is brave enough to leave. Then the rest of us will follow behind. Those of us here on this row will regroup with our white friends, but there is no reason to carry the discussion outside these auditorium doors. We have already reached a conclusion—our white friends will never agree with or even want to know what we're thinking here on this row. There's no reason to try to force them. Perhaps we don't want them to know what we're really thinking either. So we'll all head off to lunch on the front lawn and bear uncomfortable conversations and misplaced laughter, the defaced *Jet* already behind us. We'll live as unified as we can. We'll be on our best behavior, make sure another incident like this never happens, so we won't have to sit and squirm and stare each other down again. The microphones are lonely at the front of the stage. There's nothing left to be said. We're waiting for the moment signifying that we've endured this long enough. But no one is ready to stand up.

We understand each other.

We don't trust each other.

We never have.

Except

Devorah Stone

We were in a park acting like kids do, fooling around, joking, getting loud. Father said, loud enough for only us to hear, "Stop it! They'll think all Jewish people are loud."

We fell silent, and none of us questioned that wisdom. It wasn't until years later that I wondered, How would anyone have known we were Jewish? We could have been Italian or Greek or Turkish or any number of ethnic groups or nationalities. And we weren't any louder than any other family. Why had we always had to act better than everyone else?

We were Jewish.

Except
On our mother's side we weren't the Yiddish-speaking, gefilte-fish-eating, borscht-belt-visiting, Joey Bishop kind of Jewish. My maternal grandparents were from Iraq.

My grandmother never called it that. She said she was from Baghdad or Babylonia. In the 1920s, one quarter of all Baghdad residents were Jewish. On Friday nights when we went over to our grandparents' house, she told us stories of

Baghdad, of how they slept on rooftops in the summer, of the strange but joyous sound women made during celebrations, and of picking fresh dates from trees.

Except

Where we were living in Vancouver, British Columbia, only a handful of Jewish families were from anywhere other than Eastern Europe or Russia. My grandparents held Sephardic services in their house, and they could barely get a minyan— ten men—to attend.

Except

Our mother was born in Bangalore, India. She told us of monkeys stealing her food, of hearing sitar music till late at night, and of meeting Nehru.

At my grandmother's house on Friday nights and on Jewish holidays, we ate chicken curry, flatbreads, and rice, and for dessert a kind of cookie called *babas* with dates inside. Grandmother and mother made their own curry, and the fragrance permeated the house for days.

Jewish people from Europe, who laced their talking with Yiddish terms and ate bland brown food, often didn't understand we were Jewish. They couldn't believe Jewish people could come from places outside Europe. We weren't the same kind of Jewish.

My brother, sister, and I grew up in Kerrisdale, a white, mostly Protestant, middle-class neighborhood on the west side of Vancouver. We ventured to the east side and Chinatown for food from the Middle East and India.

We made some attempts to fit in, but white bread stuck to our teeth and Kool-Aid tasted vile. The Christmas tree felt like a strange creature in our house for the week we tolerated it, and after a couple years, we dropped that.

We were looked upon as freaks, and children weren't shy in saying so to our faces and taunting us as we walked home. So many things were assumed: We must be stingy or dirty or just plain weird. Our elementary school did little to stop the taunts and the teasing.

In every public school we attended, we were the sole ethnic minority. In those days, school began with the Lord's Prayer and a short Bible reading. During the New Testament readings I left the classroom.

There just wasn't anyone else who looked like us. We represented the other people of the world. Later on, I was the one to explain civil unrest, as though I represented everything that wasn't white or Christian. We didn't believe that the sun would never set on the British Empire. We didn't believe that everything British was better. We didn't stand up for "God Save the Queen."

Except

We were more English than anyone. Father was English, though his family came from Russia. And even on our mother's exotic side, we were so much like the English. In Baghdad, during World War I, her family helped the British get rid of the Turks in every way they could. They harbored British soldiers and passed information. Grandpa told us stories of thwarting the hated Turks in favor of the English army, even supplying English officers with moonshine. My grandmother told me how, as a young girl, she threw stones at the retreating Turkish army.

When my grandfather left Baghdad, it was to go to British India, where he opened up clothing stores and factories. During World War II, my grandparents opened their home to many British soldiers.

My mother, aunts, and uncles all went to British schools in India and spoke English to everyone, even to their parents.

Except

My mother's family wasn't British. They were privileged non-British people. When they left India, they came to Canada, another Commonwealth country with British institutions.

I tried to tell other people the stories of my family that filled my childhood. The stories seemed strange, different, and at times confusing, but they were all part of who I was. I had to tell them to other people, who only knew of these places from maps.

Explaining my background to the world got a little easier in high school, because everything changed.

In the mid-'60s, all kinds of people moved to Vancouver; even Kerrisdale changed. With an influx of people from India, curry houses sprang up everywhere, and my family wasn't so exotic. Canada had a new flag. We no longer had to say the Lord's Prayer at the beginning of the school day, and the Bible readings were dropped. No one sang "God Save the Queen." Being British wasn't important anymore, and the English in Canada became just as much a minority as anyone else.

Except

My brother, sister, and I weren't sure where we fit into the growing multicultural scene. We took different approaches to the question of our diverse roots. My brother decided being Jewish was the most important aspect of his identity. He immersed himself in a European Orthodox group, and even learned Yiddish. My sister embraced the Eastern Sephardic side of her roots. She learned Spanish, since some of our mother's ancestors might have come from Spain. She support-ed the causes of Jews from Syria and Ethiopia and took up the cause of many other oppressed people around the world.

I studied all my identities and many others. I studied the origins of all human beings from Africa and beyond. I decided that everything I am is important.

The Teach-In

Mary C. Lewis

"**Y**ou're staying out of school," my father told us one Monday morning, shoving a stare around the breakfast table.

My mother added quickly, "We're boycotting." Her face begged us not to talk back or question our father. If we had, he would have exploded, wrecking breakfast with his shouts and whacks and anger.

Before we could ask him to explain, my father headed off to work, and my mother herded Greg, Berry, Vivian, and me into the dining room, usually saved for special meals. Set before each chair were pencils and notebook paper. Instead of the platters and serving bowls at Thanksgiving, Christmas, and other holidays, newspapers and magazines were spread along the center of the table.

"A boycott," my mother explained, "shows disapproval, puts a stop to things as they're usually done."

"So I can boycott chores!" Berry said, running around the room. "Boycott! Boycott!" he yelled, as though the Good Humor truck had ding-a-linged and he wanted ice cream.

I held back the giggle tickling the inside of my mouth. This was not a time for playing around, my mother said, waving us all into chairs. Each morning for the next five days, she told us, we would have a "teach-in." Each afternoon, we would keep up with our regular studies. A groan trudged around the table and stopped at Greg. His face wore a big brother's smugness. What did he know that the rest of us didn't?

"There used to be a law in Montgomery, Alabama, that forced Negroes to sit in the back of the bus," my mother said. "Nine years ago, in 1955, Negroes there began a bus boycott." She opened a copy of *Ebony* magazine and pointed to a picture of a Negro woman wearing glasses and a Sunday hat and coat.

The woman was Rosa Parks, she said. "Mrs. Parks was arrested in 1955 when she wouldn't give up her seat on a bus to a white man. Do any of you know why Negroes in Montgomery felt they had to have a bus boycott?"

None of us answered. This was the first time my mother, a schoolteacher, had ever drawn us into a classroomlike give-and-take.

Finally, Greg said, "They shouldn't have to sit in the back of the bus." He sounded calm and sure. Maybe he knew to say that because he was sixteen, six years older than I was. Or maybe he'd learned about the bus boycott the summer before last, when he and my father took part in the March on Washington.

My mother continued talking, about Dr. King leading the bus boycott and the 381 days it took Negroes in Montgomery to bring about "desegregation." I wondered whether we needed desegregation in Chicago. Mostly I walked places or rode in my father's car. My mother took the bus to work because she wouldn't learn to drive a car. The few times I had ridden a bus, no one told me where to sit. It hadn't entered my mind that some folks couldn't afford cars, as my mother was explaining, or that some grownups could tell other grownups what they could and could not do. I thought only children got ordered around.

Turning the pages of *Ebony*, my mother stopped at a photograph of Negroes standing next to some cars. "During the Montgomery boycott, a lot of people got to work by sharing rides. Suppose this picture showed 42,000 Negroes who didn't ride the bus—didn't pay the 20 cents for a round-trip fare. On one day, how much money would Montgomery's bus company not receive from those 42,000 Negroes?"

After a lot of scribbling and grunting and frowning, one of us announced the answer: $8,400—a huge amount, to my mind.

"That's power," said my mother, holding each of us in a stare. When she got to me, the force of her meaning drove straight from her head to mine.

Eight thousand, four hundred dollars packed a wallop, especially if 42,000 Negroes used that amount to show they wouldn't stand for unfairness. That afternoon, as I worked on multiplication problems, I pictured cars crammed with people, riding down a big street and holding up the money that was theirs to spend as they pleased.

❧

On Tuesday, my mother told us she was going back to work the next day. The family couldn't afford the loss of money if she stayed home all week. When she told us, Berry and Vivian shared a grin; without her around, they counted on goofing off. "Starting tomorrow, Greg will lead the teach-in," my mother added. She placed a hand on his shoulder and warned, "There *will* be a test on Friday."

Ignoring Vivian's and Berry's poked-out mouths, she then laid a map of Chicago on the dining room table, unfolded it, and told us to find our neighborhood. We hunched over the map, naming places we'd visited: the Field Museum, the Museum of Science and Industry, downtown's State Street stores. After a while Greg found Chatham, in the middle of a big section below downtown.

"This is where almost all the city's Negroes live." My mother swept her hand below and then to the left of downtown and Lake Michigan. Then she pointed above downtown. "This is where almost all the whites live. The only exceptions, just about, are *here, here,* and *here.*" She jabbed a finger at 35th Street, 55th Street, and 95th Street, to the far left of the lake. "Why are so much of the south and west sides Negro, while the north side is white?" The sharpness in her eyes matched her voice, making me nervous. Her look and sound reminded me of my father.

"The mayor lives on the south side," Greg said, butting in with a contrary example, though he sounded less sure than on Monday.

"Mayor Daley lives in Bridgeport. It's all white." My mother's eyes hardened.

"What about Mr. Homan and his daughter?" I asked. "It wasn't until he died that she moved away from our block. They're both, uh . . ."

"Yes, they're white." My mother filled in a word I had trouble saying.

Berry added, "The Chinese family with the takeout place? They live near us."

"And my friend Carole," Vivian added, "her mother's white. They live around the corner from us. There's another family like that in the next block—what's their name?"

My mother studied the ceiling and let out a sigh. "Every rule," she said carefully and slowly, "has exceptions. You need to see things as they really are."

She circled the dining room. "Whites and Negroes usually aren't allowed to live in the same neighborhoods. It's unfair and it's against the law. That's not all. The public schools that white children attend get everything they need for a good education. Schools with Negro children get leftovers— if we get anything." Almost shouting, she spoke of old text-books, no textbooks, worn-out gym equipment, science labs without supplies.

"That's not right!" She smacked the table.

I'd never seen her so angry. My schoolbooks' ripped pages, the playground's broken swings, my parents' complaints about Greg's chemistry class: I'd taken all of it for granted. I thought every kid in Chicago suffered, for reasons I had never bothered to guess.

"We pay for public education through our taxes," my mother went on to say. "Whites should not have things better than Negroes. That's *racism*."

In my head, I colored a map of Chicago. Downtown was green, for money; to its right was blue, for Lake Michigan; above the green was white; below and to its left was brown. The schools in the brown places were raggedy and crummy. Would our school boycott do as much as staying off buses did for Negroes in Montgomery?

"One week isn't enough to force the school system to change," my mother said, as if reading my thoughts. "But the boycott shows how much people want things to change."

She held up yesterday's *Defender*. A headline announced that 200,000 Negro children were staying home from school. That was good, but was it good enough?

"Sacrifice," she said. She circled the table again. "Negroes in Montgomery walked to work or shared rides. You're sacrificing, too, spending only half your usual time on schoolwork so you can learn something equally important. When these five days are over, nothing should be like it was before."

Later, I did feel different as I worked on my regular studies—as though my mother had become a pumice stone and was scraping off some of my worn-out thoughts. New thoughts were forming.

For the next two days, our classroom moved to the basement. Down there, our magazines, newspapers, and school supplies could stay in sloppy piles—we didn't have to obey the rule that the dining room should stay neat. Going downstairs went with part of Tuesday's teach-in, about the Underground Railroad. That day, my mother had taught us that along the way to freedom, Negroes escaping from slavery sometimes came across "engineers" who hid them in cellars and barns. She'd told us that the Emancipation Proclamation and the Thirteenth and Fourteenth Amendments to the Constitution made us citizens as much as anyone else born in the United States. Our sacrifice on Wednesday and Thursday was to sit on metal folding chairs in the damp basement instead of soft seats in the sunny dining room.

"Dr. George Washington Carver," Greg began on Wednesday, clearing his throat, "found lots of ways to use peanuts."

"Yeah," Berry said, "peanut butter, peanut brittle, peanuts in a candy bar . . ."

"Shut up, boy," Greg warned. "Mom's going to test you on Friday."

"Quit being silly," Vivian told Berry. "This is a *teach-in.*"

A parade from Negro history stepped forward. Dr. Carver discovered things to do with and make from peanuts that helped save Southern farming. Dr. W. E. B. Du Bois, a very smart man, studied at Harvard University and the University of Berlin. In 1872, Elijah McCoy invented something so important for railroads that workers demanded "the real McCoy." Greg kept going. We memorized the Negro National Anthem, "Lift Every Voice and Sing." We recited Paul Laurence Dunbar's poem "When Malindy Sings." I heard railroad men shouting, "Give us the real McCoy!" I smelled rich dirt and roasted peanuts in Dr. Carver's hands. I sat beside Mr. Dunbar while he wrote a beautiful poem. The big, proud parade lifted me onto its shoulders.

On Thursday, my mother and I were in the kitchen making dinner. "Mom," I asked, "tell me about Birmingham."

"You mean the four little girls? Didn't Greg tell you about them?"

"Yes . . ." Earlier that day, when Greg talked about the September 15, 1963, church bombing in Birmingham, Alabama, that killed four girls, he left out the underneath part: *Why?*

My mother started making salad while naming the four girls. Cynthia Wesley: *Whack* went a knife against a row of carrots. Addie Mae Collins and Carole Robertson: *Rip, rip,* went a head of lettuce against a grater. And little Denise McNair: My mother scooped up the lettuce and carrots and let them fall into a mixing bowl. They looked like green and orange rain falling onto an earth turned inside out. The day those four girls died, did everything become topsy-turvy? I stood over the garbage can, pulling away an onion's crinkled skin, and I pictured an exploding bomb burning a child's skin. Whoever planted that bomb was hateful. I wanted to take a crayon and color Montgomery and Birmingham and the entire South blood red—the color of evil.

My eyes stung; my throat swelled. Those girls shouldn't have died. I reached for a knife. My mother fussed I was too young to slice the onion, and told me to quit wiping my eyes with hands stained by onion juice.

"Wash your hands." She shoved her fingers into the salad. "It's a shame what low-life rednecks can do to a sacred place like the Sixteenth Street Baptist Church."

"White people are mean," I said, grabbing a jar of mayonnaise.

My mother turned to me. "What about your Aunt Helen?" she asked.

I put the mayonnaise on the counter and thought about Uncle Joe's wife. Aunt Helen was white; she seemed okay. She scolded like every mother I knew, when kids messed up her carpet with dirty shoes. When I visited her, Uncle Joe, and my cousins Gerri and Derek, she roasted hot dogs and took the time to steam the buns. Was Aunt Helen secretly mean, or was she another exception to the rules?

"*Some* whites are mean," my mother said, "and some aren't." She had me look up "ignorance" in a dictionary.

"'Lack of learning or information,'" I read aloud. "So . . . they're stupid."

"They've been taught poorly," my mother said with a small smile, adding mayonnaise to the salad. "They're not all ignorant. What about Eleanor Roosevelt?"

My attention drifted back over the morning. In 1939, I remembered Greg saying, a group of white women, Daughters of the American Revolution, blocked a Negro woman, Marian Anderson, from singing at Constitution Hall in Washington, D.C. Greg said that Eleanor Roosevelt and Harold Ickes, two white people, got Miss Anderson's performance moved to the Lincoln Memorial. I asked why they helped Miss Anderson.

My mother pushed aside the salad. "Miss Anderson was a classical singer—a contralto of great renown. What a magnificent voice."

"Do you have any of her records? Can I listen to them sometime?"

She nodded and tapped her hand against the bowl. An absentminded *ping, ping,* her wedding ring hitting the bowl, accompanied the dreamy look on her face. Where had she gone, I wondered—to a concert where Marian Anderson had sung? In our family room were lots of jazz albums featuring Count Basie, Earl Hines, Duke Ellington, and Ella Fitzgerald, the "queen of scat." My father called them the "reigning royalty." Sometimes he let Greg play doo-wop 45s. But I'd never heard Marian Anderson's songs played in our home.

"Miss Anderson was praised all over the world." My mother sounded sad and angry. "But the DAR tried to stand in the way of her gift. They didn't believe Negroes deserved the treatment that whites took for granted. Here in the United States, racism tried to silence her beautiful voice."

She picked up a wooden spoon and stirred the salad. "Eventually, her gift was recognized here." She pointed the spoon at me. "Some whites have risked their lives for equality and justice. Greg told you about the Freedom Riders, didn't he?"

We talked about them as she finished making dinner. That morning we had seen magazine photos of people sitting side by side at lunch counters, people locked up in jail, people marching along city streets and country roads. Some whites in the photos had bloody faces—clubbed, my mother said, by policemen willing to hurt them, too.

Sacrifices: giving up time, safety, acceptance—whatever it took to stand up for people's right to ride a bus or eat a meal or sing on a stage. My staying home from school was small compared to what other people had gone through. I felt my back straighten and my jaw set.

That Friday, when my mother got home from work, she tested us on what we'd learned, just like she'd promised. We took the test in the dining room. She didn't explain the change, although coming back to the dining room now felt special.

Before the test, my mother placed our dictionary and *World Book* encyclopedia volumes on the table, and she dared us to find in those books the Negroes she and Greg had introduced to us. When we could find neither Du Bois, Carver, nor McCoy—almost no important Negroes—she said, "Do you see? We keep getting left out. That's why you've been having the teach-in. Your father and I want you to know the truth."

I got the highest score. I correctly answered questions about slavery, Rosa Parks, Martin Luther King, the Freedom Riders, desegregation, four girls killed in a Birmingham church, and other people and events. But the special week was not over.

On Friday night, I could not sleep. I should have felt good since I'd done so well on the test. I'd shown what I'd learned for five days about the world outside my door. No one could accuse me of ignorance. But that night, when I thought of the world inside my home, it was hard to feel sure of what I knew.

Thoughts of my father kept me awake. My mother had said he wanted us to know the truth about race relations. I had no reason to doubt it. He was the one who announced our boycott. He was the one who'd taken Greg to the March on Washington, to hear Dr. King speak about a faith the country badly needed. But another side of my father promised a fight if you questioned his rules or his commands. When Greg, Berry, or Vivian disobeyed him, he beat them. I thought, too, about how my mother tried to keep peace, tried to stay out of his way. I thought about the Marian Anderson records she never played. I turned over, thinking of my father, the good guy. Not long before the school boycott, a friend of my father—another Negro fireman—had visited. I overheard the man tell my mother, "Ozzie told 'em they had no right giving us the worst schedules. He wouldn't let them give us the short end of the stick." That was a side of my father to hold on to: a sturdy protector of fairness.

When I was younger, I remembered, I'd found his diploma, from Colored High School. I'd said, "How come there's no name? A *name,* like Washington or Franklin—any name at all?"

Something really sad and mean had burst from his eyes. Raising his fists, he'd yelled, "Stay out of my things!" That was a side of my father to run from: a hard, angry ruler of our home.

Trying to see all of him was tough. Sometimes he yelled at me, and beat my sister and brothers, but he also refused to take us to the South for summer vacations because, he told us, no child of his would drink from a water fountain labeled

"Colored." Had racism and ignorance made him a confusing mixture of really good and not good at all? Where did the fault lie for his tough, wooden side that caught fire at our tiniest mistakes? Should I blame the entire country? Did my mother's knowledge of Negro history and civil rights help her to love my father? Should I do that, learn as much as she knew, so I could love all of him, too?

Do you see? My mother said during a boycott I took part in when I was ten. *Nothing should be like it was before.* She was right: I saw things differently. Returning to school, I learned that most of my classmates had stayed home, but kept at regular studies or acted like they were on vacation. At school we never spoke of Negroes' absence from textbooks, and we didn't talk about the boycott's purpose. Aside from getting eyeglasses—a big event for me—fifth grade continued as before. The desegregation of Chicago's schoolchildren would take six more years to begin. Desegregation of teachers wouldn't begin until 1980.

Looking back on 1964 brings up a period of emerging clarity. I was learning to see why certain events deserved notice on the path of history. An equally significant truth was surfacing that year. When my mother involved me in a teach-in, I doubt she realized she was helping me grasp more than civil rights and black history. In 1964, I began to recognize the righteousness of fair, humane treatment. I also began a sketch of my father: a man proud to be black, whose facets included the very behaviors he hated. In the years to come, I would have to dig further to understand why those facets could exist in him.

Beat the Buddha Day

Colleen Nakamoto

Mileage log. Resource binder. My portable lunch—chicken teriyaki, *onigiri*, carrot sticks, apple juice—packed in a mini-cooler. Cell phone. My human heart. I am armed to face my day.

As a traveling hospice counselor, I've learned the least-trafficked routes of L.A., between Kaiser Sunset and the zip-code zones of the people I serve: 90016, 90018, 90043, 90044. I also know which homes to visit in the mornings, and which are safe for me later in the day. As a native Angelena, more specifically, as a third-generation Japanese American Angelena, I have grown up with a nose for both safety and danger. Arlington is a good street to travel, although the Robinsons live closer to Western. I drive southbound through the major intersections—Pico, Venice, Washington.

Once I cross the Santa Monica Freeway overpass, the sensitivities of my antennae heighten, the ones most receptive to an interior wave, to my own historical frequency, where degrees of color and threat intersect.

Adams, Jefferson, Exposition.

Rodeo, 39th, King.

My breathing shallows.

❧

In June 1975, Audubon Junior High's post-earthquake structures sit sober-faced, stone-bodied, like prison blocks awaiting new inmates. The invisible fences of Santa Barbara Avenue to the north, Stocker Street to the south, bind the compound. The spinal cord of the neighborhood, Crenshaw Boulevard, carries the nerve impulses of the community from its mind to its body and back, six blocks to the west.

L.A. County has not yet passed the ordinance renaming Santa Barbara Avenue as Martin Luther King Jr. Boulevard.

On the steps of the Lincoln Memorial in 1963, the Rev. Dr. Martin Luther King Jr. sang his prayer.

In 1975, it is still a dream. And while Rev. Dr. King's words resonate deeply with me, here in my skin I am neither Black nor White, which leaves me in a precarious place. In times to come, I will try to discern if and where I belong in his dream. I cannot call upon him in June of 1975, as he was murdered seven years prior. In times to come, I will have my own dream.

Audubon aches as its student body takes on a new shape, faster than its conscience, the adults in the school and community, can track.

Throb. Twist. Coil. Kick.

It begins, just outside the east gate. I'm not *on* the merry-go-round; I'm in the *center* of it, and all the dizzying horses are students. Asians, mostly Buddhaheads. And Blacks.

It's the last day of school. And while this particular tradition has gone on for at least four years, always on the last day, my parents, like the Teruyas, the Nishiokas, and the Nakayamas, send me through its gates just the same.

I go to my classes—geometry, French. At recess, I line up at the candy store window with my friends, to buy Bottle Caps and Now 'n' Laters. Report cards are a done deal, I've cleared out my locker, and it's down to a couple of last-class parties and *El Patio* signings. Rapidograph artwork and block-lettered doodling, formerly reserved for PeeChee covers, join well-wishes from friends in the leaves of my yearbook.

I deny what awaits me at the three o'clock bell. This is rooted in either innocence or arrogance, or in that distinctly junior high concoction, a swirling potion of both. Although I'd witnessed this phenomenon last year, from behind Mr. Nakayama's windshield, denial is an animal that loves to be fed.

Clocked.

It's the last bell of the year, after which no one can be suspended. I exit the gate and find my carpool group—Emi, Monique, Lori, and Jan—waiting at our usual spot on the lawn. I find them, and in that moment, I lose something, too. My world starts to spin, a Kodak slide carousel shorting out, shooting rapid fire.

Kevin Katsuyama. Two Black guys in his face, shoving his chest, his shoulders. His lips, pursed together as if he's holding back the force of his life. They're talking major smack to him, "Whatcha gon' do about it, *Buddha?*" He's holding his PeeChee and *El Patio* in front of his groin. Turning slightly to the right.

Steven Kuratsu. Suddenly flat on the grass, face down. Three Black guys yelling at him, daring him to stand up, jumping around the way boxers do in the ring. When he tries to get up, one of them stomps down, square in the center of his back. Hard. Steven fights for breath. His hands grab at the grass. He can't get up. They're laughing.

Mike Uyemura. Bookin' down the street, *damn* he's running fast. Five or six Black guys, one of them gripping a shovel, its spade pointed toward the sky—they're chasing him. Mike's the prize Asian guy to whup, because he usually takes shit from no one, and he's fast, he's built, even in eighth grade. A Buddhahead O. J. Simpson.

Kevin, Steven, and Mike are three of the many Sansei boys I've grown up with in Crenshaw. Depending on the week or the phase of the moon, either they are engaged in crushes on my friends or they're bugging us with their silly jokes and antics. It isn't until now I realize we look out for each other, too, and in this moment, they are my brothers. They are my brothers and I stand paralyzed as they are hunted down, humiliated, punched, and kicked, right in front of my face.

For a split second, I remember that my brother's friend Neil was hit on his head with a lead pipe this day four years ago, and was rushed to the hospital.

A fractured skull. Rivulets of blood snaking through fissures. Hidden. Unexposed.

How or why this ritual began, circa 1970, has never been discussed or formally determined. Over the years, I have generated my hypotheses, in accordance with my own processes of healing and growth. Back then, as a thirteen-year-old, I simply knew that being Asian increased my vulnerability—vulnerability to being harassed, vulnerability to being jumped. In college, I grew to believe that this particular minority of Black kids had probably become fed up with the differences in the ways the faculty treated Asian students and Black students. While I had no specific recollection of preferential treatment, I reconciled the assaults with a naive sense of generalization and guilt—and believed that perhaps we should have challenged the favoritism. I wondered if we'd brought this upon ourselves, by being who we were. If we were somehow responsible. I tried to make sense of the images that haunted me.

❧

Emi, standing two feet away from me. And that rowdy-ass Black girl, Trina, who once cornered me in the stairwell for money. She'd stopped me in the shadows and kept moving closer and closer, saying, "Hey, you got some money? Give me your money." I drew a quarter and a dime from my pocket. "I only have thirty-five cents." Trina's friend said, "*Tsk,* shut up, Trina, leave that girl alone; she's cool." Trina *tsk*'d back, and they walked on. I don't remember completing the errand I was on for Miss Meadows, only how lonely the stairway felt, how cold the concrete was.

Now, Trina and her no-name sidekick, all up in Emi's face, talking smack. Emi, returning a glare but no words. Trina, circling Emi like she's territory, prey, then shoving her hard from the back. Emi, stumbling forward, shouting, "Stop it!" Monique, standing next to Emi. Me, wondering if anything will happen to Monique; she's Black. Wondering in a flash if she's protected. Or, perhaps, marked.

No one touches me or gets directly in my face, but the vibe of this mania is rapid, rabid, staccato. I'm frozen on my feet, turning my head just enough to scan for proximity and degree of danger. I command my voice to stay in, my body to remain upright, not to shake or call attention to myself. I immediately value, and wield, my puny size. It becomes my best defense. It becomes my weapon.

This is where I learn to disappear.

Trina's in Emi's face again, but thank God, Mr. Nakayama's brown Riviera is pulling up. Though I don't remember moving, Emi and Monique are sitting in front, and Lori, Jan, and I are in the back. And Trina's getting her face in the window on the driver's side, yelling crazy shit straight in Mr. Nakayama's face, "Whatchou lookin' at, mothafucka? Come here, I'll kick your ass, too!" She kicks his car. I can't believe it. He yells back at her, then hits the accelerator. I can't remember what he said. I don't see the teachers or grownups from school anywhere.

Two blocks ahead, I see Cynthia Yee. She's Chinese American, but that doesn't matter. She's marked as a prize to jump, just like Mike. She and her cousin Donna are surrounded by a group of girls. Cynthia is slamming her books on the ground, yelling. I see the shiny scream of her braces, and the wild motions of her arms, like the wings of a trapped falcon. I see her through the front windshield, through the side window, through the back windshield.

There is nothing random about this attack; it feels too thorough, too pervasive. As we drive down Ninth Avenue toward Santa Barbara, I see a frenzy of Asian and Black bodies, whole and yet strangely piecemeal, flying in the streets.

⤙❧⤚

I wasn't totally new to violence against Asians in Crenshaw. In 1967, while waiting in line outside my first grade classroom after lunch, a fifth-grade girl grabbed me by the wrist. "Did you wash your hands yet? Come with me." Once in the empty bathroom, she cornered me in a stall, put her hands around my neck, and squeezed. All I remember are her eyes, the pain and madness there, and my inability to scream or breathe, because of the force of her thumbs pressing into my throat. I told no one about it. Not my teachers, not my parents. By first grade, I'd learned the nature of random threat; I'd also created my own coping strategy: No Words = No Reality. I'd learned to swallow trauma.

In 1972, Mr. and Mrs. Nakamura had been gagged and tied to the chairs in their family room by two men who'd broken into their home. I remember feeling as though I wasn't supposed to find out about it.

And in 1974, my mom had been jumped in the Food Giant parking lot on Crenshaw and Coliseum (a half mile north of where the Magic Johnson Theatres now stand). Her purse was ripped off her arm, and when she woke up on the asphalt, all she saw was sky. Sky, and a man and woman sitting in their car, just watching her.

I was the only one home when she pulled up in her station wagon. She walked in with her dark glasses on, and said, "Oh, I was *assaulted*." I didn't exactly know what "assaulted" meant, but I knew she wasn't acting like my mom. It was as though she were lost in midair, ashamed in shock's boots, a green-black-brown pond growing a ring around her arm to match what would blossom above her cheek—Saturn, soiled and bending. And I did not know what to do. Back then, your teachers would tell you how to get under tables, tuck your head down and turn away from the transoms in case of emergency, but they just didn't teach you what to do if your mom got *assaulted*.

These incidents were not necessarily isolated, but neither did they happen en masse. However, this particular annual Beat the Buddha Day (its official name, even before I'd arrived at Audubon) was an organized initiation, a premeditated rite of passage. Passage from behind insulating windshields and hearsay, to fists and flesh, to rakes, chains, and shovels. Passage off school property, onto the streets of collective assault.

Our parents never registered complaints about this to the school, to local law enforcement, or to the media. Perhaps some never even knew. This color-on-color violence never made the evening news.

Most of my parents' generation, the Nisei, had been ordered to live in U.S. internment camps during World War II. They emerged, knowing in dark, unspoken places that the principles and practices of justice, for them, were to exist in word but not in deed; the system was not theirs to fall back on. Our Nikkei community learned to suck it up, and move on.

But you can only suck it up so far. The Nikkei were not alone in this knowledge. When people are enslaved or incarcerated, are used and discarded, or struggle for generations with sociopolitical tentacles stamping them as unwanted, their life force needs somewhere to go, some way to claim they are still human and alive. Some communities reposition, restrategize; others implode.

Many of our parents coped, when it came time for us to attend high school, by gaining transfer permits from Dorsey to Westchester. How strange yet somehow understandable it was, the way some of the Buddhahead kids felt more at home with the Black transfer students from Morningside than we did with our new White peers from the sands of Playa del Rey. Buddhaheads and Blacks, now outsiders to a strange and powerful host culture, tried to trace our ways home on the topographies of each other's skin. Our familiarities with one another, even across memory fences of pain, equipped us with points of reference, even strength and identity, from which to navigate, to retool for the new demands of survival. This larger world, the Westchester campus, was clearly owned by the sea of White faces all around us, many of whom had the look, the look betraying no doubt about their right to walk upon the earth. And yet, some of us, tired and burned by the past, gravitated toward our new and novel cohorts, discovering both commonalities and differences we'd carry forth into our expanding worlds. History became dynamic; for some, it was a new day of unlikely alliances.

I know now, in this phase of my evolution, that Beat the Buddha Day was a desperate ritual of implosion. Audubon Junior High was emblematic, spokes on a color wheel of the unwanted. I veer away from the scent of political correctness, which might intellectualize or rationalize all that had happened. I acknowledge the pressing, historical context of the Civil Rights Movement. But I also acknowledge that no opportunity was ever provided to us as students to debrief these annual tragedies. No one described how we Asian kids may have been repeatedly targeted as stand-ins for a dominant, oppressive culture. No one taught us that a parallel Yellow Power movement was hard at work, up and down Crenshaw. No one told us that communities of color were uniting, not dividing, and finding common ground.

I acknowledge these macrorealities.

I also insist that it was horrific. I insist that too many of us, the Asian American students of Audubon Junior High—twelve-, thirteen-, and fourteen-year-olds—were unjustly terrorized, violated, and victimized by our fellow students and community members. I insist that a large portion of the travesty was the re-victimization that occurred through the community's silence, ironically proportionate to the level of trauma. This served nearly to sanction what had happened, relegating Beat the Buddha Day to a place of helplessness and shame in our memories, feeding an internal, emotional cancer. I also insist that it has taken years, in a world of racial otherness—being neither Black nor White—to come to terms with all that went down. We've had no communal language to explain what happened. We've known no recourse, save moving away and hoping that either physical or mental distance would serve as an adequate eraser.

Today, Leimert Park is a landmark in the Crenshaw District, a nexus for L.A.'s African American cultural renaissance. The World Stage stands, an elastic, reverberating three blocks from those east gates of Audubon. It is a place for new artistic genius to be discovered and nurtured; it stands for empowerment and for the affirmation of voice. I celebrate this reality. At the very same time, in weaker moments, I feel Leimert's old ghosts laughing, ready to mark me and my Asian face all over again, were I ever to return to its streets.

The power of body memory.

The aftertaste of silence.

Now, two hundred blocks to the south, and just three blocks to the east, I sit near the southern tip of Crenshaw, that sloping cord of history. I wonder, What will be resurrected in this renaissance? Which annual holidays?

My dream is a simple one. I light a candle for acknowledgment, for the untying of throats, the opening of mouths, and the spilling forth of stories—scarred, mighty, and true.

Bottle Caps.

Now 'n' Laters.

Beat the Buddha Day.

Mirror

Karen Elias

Where were you when JFK was shot? Where were you when a man landed on the moon? When Martin Luther King Jr. was shot? Malcolm shot? When the Rodney King verdict announced? Where were you when Emmett Till floated up to the surface of the Tallahatchie River for Bye-bye Babying *a white woman?*

—JOHN EDGAR WIDEMAN, "Looking at Emmett Till"

On Saturday mornings in 1954, if you are a white girl living in the suburbs, you can sit at your vanity table and memorize your face. You can divide it into its separate parts, hold your hand over one side, then the other, testing for symmetry. You can practice smiling to see whether the same number of teeth appears at right and left of center. Pressing your fingers against the bump at the top of your nose, you can try your best to smooth it into oblivion, to make this face in front of you in the mirror the perfect face, exactly like the one you draw obsessively in study hall, with its blue eyes, turned-up nose, and flawless white skin. If you are susceptible to romantic conceits, you can superimpose the vacant planes of this perfect face over your own less-than-perfect one and eventually convince yourself that, with a little pluck and patience—raising your chin just so, combing your hair just so—it might be possible to erase everything that makes you interesting and turn yourself into this likeness: fashion model, trophy girl, cheerleader, cartoon.

The racial landscape in America has begun to change. Over the next few years, President Eisenhower, a conservative interested in courting white Southern votes, will refuse to support *Brown v. Board of Education,* will resist its implementation, and will express regret at his appointment of Justice Earl Warren to the Supreme Court. Over the next few years, Southern states will increasingly find ways to defy the new ruling—by shutting down schools ordered to desegregate or by funding segregated private education—and Eisenhower will merely turn his back. Sometime before *Brown* is made into law, during the Supreme Court's preliminary deliberations on segregation, Eisenhower invites Earl Warren to the White House. After dinner, he puts his hand on Warren's arm. "These are not bad people," he says, speaking of the Southern segregationists. "All they're concerned with is to see that their sweet little girls are not required to sit in school alongside some big, overgrown Negroes."

In 1954, you are fourteen, a year older than Emmett Till. The next summer, Emmett, called Bo by his family, visits relatives in Mississippi, where he is beaten to death by two white men, Roy Bryant and J. W. Milam, because (they claim) he has forgotten his place with a white woman while buying bubblegum at a local grocery store. The two men, who eventually admit to murdering him, are acquitted by an all-male, all-white jury, whose members take only one hour and seven minutes to reach a verdict. After his acquittal, Milam, in an interview, recalls telling Emmett that he is tired of progressives sending agitators down South to cause trouble and that he intends to make an example of him. For many, Emmett Till's murder marks the beginning of the Civil Rights Movement. John Lewis, a civil rights activist, talks about this time: "The Till case galvanized the country. A lot of us young black students in the South later on, we weren't sitting in just for ourselves—we were sitting in for Emmett Till. We went on Freedom Rides for Emmett Till."

As the nightly news focuses more frequently on racial protests and counterprotests, the insulating effect of the suburbs, within which your family has been able to maintain a temporary protective façade, begins to wear thin. Your father issues pronouncements at the dinner table. He makes it clear that, without the presence of communist-inspired outside agitators, none of this would be happening. On this, he and your mother are in complete agreement. Until *Brown,* things were working fine. Negroes were perfectly satisfied with their condition. Up to now race was never an issue, so why call attention to it? Isn't America, after all, a great melting pot, a welcoming place where anyone—given the proper motivation—can achieve resounding prosperity? Take our own family as an example, your father says. Odds were against us one hundred percent, and just look where we are now. With no help from anyone.

Sometimes your father breaks the ensuing silence with an attempt at humor. More and more often the typical dinner-table joke, which inadvertently reveals his belief in a so-called natural social hierarchy, now features three men in a leaky boat: a white man, a Jew, and a Negro. The white person, because he has the larger, more enlightened perspective, always manages to escape unharmed. Your father is ambivalent about Jewish people, those who occupy the next rung down on his social ladder. Although some have clear affiliations with communism, he admires their motivation. They own houses in the more affluent neighborhoods, and for the most part they keep their religious identity to themselves. It is those who refuse to assimilate, who speak Yiddish or wear yarmulkes, who call attention to their Jewishness like the man in the joke, who are doomed to fall overboard.

The black man, in your father's world, never has a chance.

Nor in your mother's. Your mother has become president and program chair of the junior high PTA. This signals a shift in her personality. The PTA has recognized considerable leadership potential in your mother. Now, her confidence buttressed by each new speech, each new challenging encounter, she is ready to claim a place, and a voice, in the world of education.

When the implications of *Brown* come home to her, your mother is incensed. She is concerned for your sister, who, unlike you, is not riding the tracking system to higher ground. Your sister has not readily taken to school and will need a push to excel, will be forced, your mother complains with increasing vehemence, to attend classes with kids bussed in from poorer sections of town. From your mother's perspective, *Brown* has single-handedly put your sister's academic future in jeopardy.

Your mother uses her position as an elected officer of the PTA to oppose desegregation. She writes a monthly column for the newsletter, makes speeches at the local and state levels in which she refines her arguments. Isn't education, in the long run, the golden key? And, as parents, haven't they worked long and hard for the right to educate their sons and daughters in the best of schools? Now a federal law, put in place by society's most "liberal elements" and over which they themselves have absolutely no control, is insisting on mixing races that have not the slightest desire to be mixed. What this law is asking is contrary to natural inclination. She knows this to be true. It has ruined everything.

Your mother never gets over the *Brown* ruling. For the remainder of her life, she will continue to believe that its mandate to desegregate marks a dividing line between a time of possibility and a time of hopeless decline. Race is the culprit, one she can never forgive. Increasingly, whenever she finds herself in the company of African Americans, she sees these meetings as opportunities—even invitations—to express her outrage once again. It's significant that she seldom discusses the ruling with anyone else. Nor does she once consider the effect of this discussion on her audience. Her listener is merely a stand-in for Race itself. Decades later, she meets her African American granddaughter-in-law for the first time.

"Now tell me," your mother says, leaning in her direction over the table at tea, "what do you think about *Brown versus Board of Education?*"

When the photographs of Emmett Till's face are published in *Jet,* you do not see them. If you were to see them, you would have to dig deep, down past outside agitators, past sad leaking boats, past the inability to recognize your whiteness in the mirror or to see your own face as marked by experience or history, before you could get to any place that could properly be called a beginning.

In your world, it is many years before Emmett Till has a chance.

Question: Where were you when Emmett Till was murdered?

Answer: Lost in a mirror. Waiting to be picked. Hoping to be called the one and only.

When Emmett Till was pulled from the Tallahatchie River, he was, according to John Edgar Wideman, nearly unrecognizable: "crushed, chewed, mutilated, his gray face swollen, water dripping from holes punched in his skull." His face, Wideman says, was a "blurred, grayish something resembling an aerial snapshot of a landscape cratered by bombs or ravaged by natural disaster."

Emmett Till carried a picture of a white girl in his wallet. His mother says it was Hedy Lamarr, a standard photo that came with the new wallet they bought together before Bo left for Mississippi. Wideman says perhaps it was another student from Chicago, a girl in a class picture smiling from the second row. Emmett, trying to show off for his country audience, perhaps pointed to her, to the prettiest white girl, the one with the most symmetrical, blue-eyed, pert-nosed face, and bragged that she was his. For his killers, this was the ultimate transgression. In an interview, J. W. Milam said, "Well, when he told me about this white girl he had, my friend, well, that's what this war's about down here now, that's what we got to fight to protect, and I just looked at him and say, Boy, you ain't never gone to see the sun come up again."

A premise at the core of racist America: this belief in sweet little white girls whose innocence we got to fight to protect. In the space of a synapse so small it was at one time nearly invisible, this assumed innocence became, in Wideman's words, the "nightmare J. W. Milam discovered in Emmett Till's wallet," the unthinking justification for his death. Hers was the face you wanted to have, the desirable face, your ticket to what you considered a normal life.

This is the girl you were in training to be.

Homecoming

Ana Chavier Caamaño

A homecoming story is told like this: The wayward traveler makes it across the world in her quest to return to the one place that holds her heart. Her family welcomes her with tearful joy and stories of what has occurred since last they saw her. The traveler also has stories, of what she has seen, learned, and become. It ends with the traveler gleefully proclaiming that of all the places in the world, of all the people she has met, of all the adventures she has lived, nothing compares to her one and only home, her blood, her family. Mine is not that story.

Traveling west with my window rolled down, I suck in the unsullied gusts of the South Dakota plains. The slight hills that lead Minnesota into South Dakota on Highway 12 rock me like a baby and then, at last, lead to peaceful, almost sleepy, flat terrain. The horizon is clear and very far away. Fields, sky, and that's all. My eye is finally able to rest without the obstructions of the buildings of San Francisco, where I have lived for four years. When I come home to see my parents,

I must first fly to Minneapolis, Minnesota, and then backtrack by car five-and-a-half hours west to Aberdeen, South Dakota. My hometown. Flying into Aberdeen is too remote and, therefore, too expensive for me.

Groton, South Dakota, sits twenty miles outside of Aberdeen. The small town's one stoplight marks the deadline to start a mental preparation for my Homecoming. My parents and childhood home await me. In some way, Aberdeen felt foreign to me all of my life. I was born and raised in Aberdeen; I lived there until I left for college. Although I'm sure I called it "escaped" back then. But now, the uneasiness that I feel rises up to meet my excitement. And as I get closer to home, my questions begin to surface, buoyant and persistent. What if the buildings don't feel familiar anymore? If they have faded into the ground, do they swallow my memories of childhood with them in order to make way for a new and unfamiliar generation's memories? The gap of time that I've been away could possibly have been much too damaging. I'd gone away from Aberdeen not wanting to own the small-town, Midwestern American–girl part of me. Am I able to call this a Homecoming at all, if I've denied this piece of me? Do I still have this right? Will the faces recognize me?

The wheat fields wave me in the right direction in case I've forgotten the way. The corn fields offer an endless green comfort to my growing anxiety. As I reach Aberdeen, I slow the car to a law-abiding, nearly impossible twenty-five miles per hour. Here all the trucks and Oldsmobiles signal their turns, and give small-town waves of "hello" as they pass by. My city-mind wonders if I know them.

Aberdeen is skewered by Highway 12. Its name changing to Sixth Avenue in town, it starts with a horse stable and ends with the Starlight Truck Stop. This town, where I stood out with my Caribbean freckles and curly hair, made a Midwestern American girl out of me. I pass the John Deere tractor sales lot; the McDonald's, where I held my first job and joked with my friends that I got the job so the establishment could fill its ethnic quota; Alexander Mitchell Library, where story time was the best baby sitter my mother could find; Roncalli High School, where I once found inscribed on my desk the words "Get back on your banana boat and go back to where you came from"; a few blocks later, the house where I attended Girl Scout meetings; and, finally, into the driveway of my childhood home. As I stepped out of my car, like a sailor returning from a long voyage, I understood the urge to kiss the ground and worship the familiarity.

The house, a 1968 rambler my parents built on the outskirts of town, is now surrounded by a thriving middle-class neighborhood. Outside, I pause, listening to the stock cars hum and whistle their way around the Brown County Fairgrounds' racetrack. The crickets chime in, as if to remind me what summer sounded like when I was a child. The South

Dakota girl in me wakes to notice that by the look of the clouds, a thunderstorm is approaching. I guess it will reach us in an hour or two.

My hand on the knob, I can already hear the merengue from Mom and Dad's stereo. It takes me back to our night-time flights into the Dominican Republic, where below us, the sporadically dispersed lights throughout the countryside lay like a golden shawl over the brown skin of the island. The cab from the airport always reeked of sweat, cheap cologne, the Caribbean Sea, and sausages, and merengue shouted from radios in the *colmados* along the highway to the capital city of Santo Domingo. The people grouped around lit-up stores, buying rum and drinking it from squishy plastic cups while sitting on their mopeds, watching us speed by in our rented transportation, my parents and four little girls, tourists, packed in with noses pressed to the windows.

Opening the door and stepping into the kitchen I am greeted by the thick smell of *arroz con pollo* and *plátanos*. The same smells of Abuela's *cocina* in Santo Domingo, where upon my arrival, a throng of aunts, uncles, and cousins would run to welcome me. But here in Aberdeen, I slip serenely into the arms of just my mother and father. The Brugal rum is on the counter waiting for the inaugural drink. My home is the moment when the cultures cross. That fleeting glimpse of change, and then the constant rock and sway of Midwest and Caribbean customs.

⁓✧⁓

As a child, I wasn't able to bridge the gap in my mind. The gap that meant I felt at home neither in Aberdeen nor in the Dominican Republic. Things fall into those gaps. Acceptance and belonging. When I was a kid, my mother would dress herself, and us, in traditional Dominican clothes and make traditional Dominican dishes for Aberdeen's International Food Festival. She decorated her booth with sea creatures, Dominican art, the flag, and a map. I was too young then to realize how our booth differed from the Scandinavian and German ones. All I knew was that traffic at our booth was very slow. Later, I didn't want to dress up, to explain myself and my family, our customs, where in the world the Dominican Republic was, what language my parents were speaking, what the smell was coming from my mother's kitchen. (How do you explain *tostones, La Bandera Dominicana,* or *pastelitos* to a fellow twelve-year-old raised on three-bean salad and not willing to try anything new?) Alternately, what I had craved in the Dominican Republic was a way to go undetected—to be seen as one of their own.

The six of us, my parents and my three sisters and I, were the only Latinos in Aberdeen, a town with a population of roughly thirty thousand. My mom and dad, both Dominican, acculturated to American ways and simultaneously tried to maintain Dominican traditions for their four daughters. They raised us to become equal parts American women and *mujeres Latinas.* What they couldn't give us was a Latino community. So they improvised, building something of a surrogate

American extended family: a German man and his Haitian wife and their children, a Chinese family, and Iranian, Finnish, Indian, and Irish families, to name a few. Together we satiated our common need for cultural understanding as we shared foods, traditions, and stories. The buffet lines at holiday parties took extra long as the chefs shared descriptions of each dish, traded recipes and traditions. A culinary feast lay sprawled before us like a relief map of the world. German pastries, Chinese vegetables, Dominican meats. And always, the ever-present thread of translation running through the cord of conversation. "How do you say 'goat' in Spanish?" "Is that a custom here?" "What do they do for Christmas Eve in the Dominican Republic?" And as the party progressed, the more the differences trickled away and left us with a festive gathering of friends celebrating together.

But this international community could not teach me my mother tongue, and because I did not know Spanish, my visits "home" to Santo Domingo were often wordless. The wall of language that stood between my family and me has been a source of frustration all my life.

My cousin Ramiro, who was closest to me in age, was often my number-one conversation partner. Eager as I was to speak Spanish, he was just as eager to hear English. Afternoons at the beach were spent with sticks in our hands, spelling words and quickly drawing their meanings in the sand, before the waves could wash away the lessons.

⁓❧⁓

In the winter of 1998, my grandmother and I sat in the dining room of her house in Santo Domingo. I approached her with a gentle voice and simple words so as not to startle her. She had gone blind from glaucoma, but her 103-year-old smile acknowledged my presence. I took her hand in silence and sat next to her.

This would be the last time I would see her. I was sure of it even as I sat there. I struggled to emboss the image on my memory of the two of us sitting in peace, together. We had just finished eating and Abuela had already taken her afternoon bath to help battle the heat. She wore her white dress for the hot Caribbean afternoon. I wanted to ask her when she had stopped wearing the mourner's black and gray. My grandfather had died more than two decades before, but I had always remembered her wearing the gray dress with the black flowers on it. In our home movies, in Aberdeen, I would often sit by myself and run the portions filmed in the Dominican Republic in slow motion, to make them last longer. I would pause, listening to the clicking of the projector, and watch the slow blinking of my aunts, uncles, cousins, and grandparents. Watching them mouth words in Spanish to the camera, slow enough even for me to be able to decode their meaning. I pretended I was there in the room, looking my young grandmother in the face. I guess in my selfish way, I had always wished it were true—that they didn't move as fast as the rest of the world, that not much would change until I got there, that they would wait for me to continue so that I wouldn't miss a thing.

As I felt her hand that day, the softness of it surprised me. She'd been a hard-working matriarch for a majority of her life. Was the Caribbean climate really that different? How rough she must have found my American hands. Our silence soaked me entirely. In the other rooms was the chaos of family—voices, music. Yet here we sat, stealing time to hang on to each other.

I wanted to explain that my biggest regret in life so far was not being able to speak fluently with my extended family, that my heart was filled with sadness that I had never been able to approach her with my little-girl joys and my young-woman troubles. Advice on love, recipes for *sancocho, pasteles, y plátanos,* directions on how to reason with my strict father (who had turned out to be very much like her husband, from what my *tías* told me), the importance of washing rice before cooking it, and the merits of being a good listener among a house full of loud *dominicanos*—all of these things lost to the rapid swirl of my struggling translation.

I touched the gold ring on her finger. It had been worn by four generations of Chavier women before being given to my grandmother. Whatever had been engraved on the face of it was now worn smooth. I felt their stories concentrated inside the gold. It looped her finger like a yarn of remembrance, creating an indentation from the pressures of the years and the tales of my family. She had known them. They knew one another's virtues, shortcomings, blessings, and tribulations. Word for word.

On our repeated visits to Santo Domingo, we always stayed long enough that my sisters and I would begin to understand the jokes and to answer the questions, but we always left too soon to retain anything once we returned to Aberdeen. "You're so dark! Say something in Spanish," my friends would beg me while marveling at my tan. And I would search nervously, for anything I could mutter. "Zapatos," I would say and offer up other strange and exotic-sounding words for everyday items like shoes and butter. Every visit to Santo Domingo would instill in me a fresh resolve, stronger each time, to keep the memories, faces, and words lodged in my brain: *I promise myself I'll remember. I swear I won't forget.*

There is a little anger in me at my parents for not letting us have that connection to our heritage. They partly regret it. I have seen it in the frustration of having to interpret for us even though we are all grown. I've taken Spanish classes. I've taken the initiative to learn more than what I absorbed on those childhood visits. The ever-present fear of failing to speak correctly kept me from using it. Or perhaps it was the eighteen years of living in a six-person Latino community, living in South Dakota, where I was often taken automatically for Native American by Midwesterners, or where, because I was

"Spanish," I was assumed to be fluent and was pressured to speak it and to get all As in Spanish class.

My eyes traced my *abuela* again. As they moved across her face, with all the questions and statements in my head, I simply muttered, *"Te amo,* Abuela."

"I love you" was all that was possible in that moment. Still, Abuela and I hadn't been alone in a room since I was a baby, and all I could muster was that. Instantly I became angry with myself, punishing myself inwardly for my cowardice. Abuela reached over, grasped both of my hands and replied, *"Te amo también,* Ana. *Te amo mucho."*

It wasn't that she said she loved me too; I already knew that. It was that she heard me and understood me. It was as if she was saying that she understood this battle that had been raging in my head all along. And that she was just waiting patiently for me to acknowledge that I could shed my inhibitions, to acknowledge to myself that I could be *dominicana* without having to back it up with words. It made me feel more at home than I'd ever felt before in South Dakota *or* Santo Domingo.

In her simple gesture, Abuela was able to unravel for me a lifetime of the confusion of being "half and half." I used to think that I had to choose, one or the other. She gave me the feeling that I can create "home" anywhere I choose it to be.

❧

Back at home, my South Dakota home, in the kitchen, my mother serves me up a plate of the "Dominican Flag": rice and beans, chicken, and plantains. She and my father proceed to gossip, catching me up on Aberdeen and family in Santo Domingo. Outside, the storm starts up, just as I thought.

Running Girl

Nnedi Okorafor-Mbachu

When I was young, I was always running. And so this Wednesday in 1982 was much like any other day back then. I was running fast, close at the heels of my two older sisters, Ngozi and Ifeoma. I was breathing hard because I was terrified. Uniform homes flew by as I ran. Red brown white bricks, white painted wood, fences recently placed around houses and backyards, and white Ford Mustangs and Datsuns with black speed stripes, and once in a while a weedy empty lot. During more peaceful moments, when I wasn't being chased by a group of young racists, I would traipse around in these places looking for what I could find.

The light-green bulbous spittlebugs were easy to find. They lived in a dollop of salivalike fluid. When they grew up, they'd be green or sometimes rainbow-colored leafhoppers. Lovely. My favorite creatures were the chunky yellow, black, red fat-butted grasshoppers and fluorescent-green katydids. These were always a treasure because they were hard to spot, let alone catch. There were also ladybugs, caterpillars, butterflies and moths, earthworms, and sometimes crayfish, toads, and frogs. Never spiders. My father always liked to hear about my day's catch. He, too, liked to witness nature. Unfortunately, because he was always on call at the hospital, he'd often hear about my day's catch late at night, long after the creatures had been freed.

At the moment, though, I wasn't at peace. I wasn't where I wanted to be at all. It was the middle of summer, eighty-five degrees, not a cloud in the sky. The sun shone brightly on exactly what was happening under it. I wore pink shorts, a rose-colored shirt, and black Chuck Taylors. My legs and arms were like toothpicks, and people at school called me Palm Tree, Nnedi Spaghetti, and Daddy Long Legs, among other less savory names.

"We're gonna get you, niggers!"

Ifeoma was ten, Ngozi was nine, and I was eight. All of the kids chasing us were in high school. The three of us had rounded a corner, on our way home from the park, when we met the group of white kids. My sisters and I froze and stared back at the seven, eight kids. The moment was a stalemate of realization. All of our schedules were about to become very modified.

The white kids were no longer going to talk shit to each other for the next fifteen minutes about why the Scorpions rocked, and my sisters and I were no longer going to take the short way home. Without a word, the three of us took off. Ifeoma leading, then Ngozi, and then me. Our shiny Jheri curls dripped oil and sweat into our eyes. I was sure in my stride, so I snuck a glance back. We would outrun them, though we were much younger. Speed ran in our family.

Our father had competed nationally in the hurdles in college. Once in a while I went with him to the track and marveled at how fast he could still run run run, leap, run run run, leap. Our mother had made the Nigerian Olympic Team by throwing the javelin, and I liked to speculate that we had warrior blood in our veins. If only I'd had a spear this particular Wednesday.

We ran down the sidewalks of South Holland, Illinois, in 1982, like my relatives before us who ran down the dirt roads of Isiekenesi and Arondizuogu, Nigeria, like my stolen relatives who ran down the dirt roads of Jackson, Mississippi. So the cycle continues.

My family was one of the first black families to move into the neighborhood, and there was a heavy price to pay for this. They threw paint into our swimming pool, forwarded hate letters to our mailbox, shouted, "Nigger, go home!" as they passed in their cars. Constant harassment.

Nevertheless, neither my sisters nor I thought much about it. It was all part of the territory. And as the daughters of confident immigrant doctors, we were taught that all ailments—physical and otherwise—could be worked with, if not cured. We were taught always to walk with our heads up and to look a scary thing in its many eyes. My parents were essentially healers; it was their job to make people feel okay, and my sisters and I were no exceptions. Their words were like vitamins to us.

"Just because someone thinks something does not make it true," my mother always said. My parents knew this well, for they came to the United States in 1969, when black people were still believed to be essentially lazy, unambitious, and slow-minded. They came with nothing, ignored these words and sentiments, and did their thing, which included earning PhDs and MDs and bringing four children into the world. No, my parents knew better than to go by old American "truths."

As we ran, something told Ifeoma to make a sharp left between two houses, and Ngozi and I quickly followed. It turned out to be a dead end. We stopped and turned to face the group. I could feel adrenaline surging up my legs to my head. I was alive and damn ready to fight. I was lanky, but that didn't matter. I'd had just about enough of this bullshit. It was like this every day. We were always running. The minute we got off the bus, we were running from white folk. We'd be walking around the block and the next minute we'd be running from white folk. On the playground. Everywhere. Something had to give.

I remembered sitting near the front of the bus and looking back when I heard someone say the word "nigger." It couldn't have been aimed at anyone else, since my sisters and I were the only blacks at Trinity grade school.

I turned around and looked down the aisle to see Cermak, the fattest kid in school, standing in front of Ifeoma. His doughy head reminded me of the *fu fu* we ate at home with *egusi* soup. But I loved *fu fu* and greatly detested Cermak. The bus had come to a halt at our stop, but Cermak was blocking Ifeoma's way. Ngozi was sitting right behind me and we both stood up.

"What are you going to do, you African nigger bitch?" he said to Ifeoma in a singsong voice. "You're just a dirty monkey and we're gonna take you to jail. Where you belong."

I gasped. Jail! Oh my God, I thought. At the time, I believed him. I knew he was wrong, but I was so scared that I believed him. My sister was going to jail! Such a terrible place. Just because she was black. In that moment, it really hit me what it meant to be black.

To be black and female meant I was ugly, helpless, a victim. Even back then, I knew this wasn't me. I listened to and agreed with my parents' sentiment that words and ideas had both power and limitations, that other people's "truths" didn't reflect my reality. Still I felt sad and disturbed that people perceived me in such stereotyped ways. And none of us could fight that evil fat boy who had been made that way by his parents, brainwashed, confused, and then initiated so early into the white man's role as king of the world.

I made eye contact with Ifeoma. She was the tallest and the most stoic. She could be very mean when she wanted to be, but she was also very protective. I could tell by the look in her eye that she wasn't scared at all. She was glad he had chosen to pick on her instead of Ngozi or me.

"Leave her alone!" Ngozi said in her high voice. She was beefier than Ifeoma and I, but she was not as imposing as Ifeoma.

"Shut up," Cermak said. He turned back to Ifeoma, drew back his hand, and slapped Ifeoma across the face. Ngozi lunged forward but a boy held her back. I looked back at the bus driver, who only watched in the rearview mirror. I turned frantically to my sister, my legs frozen. I was too skinny and small to fight him. And his several friends were too big.

"Where is my daughter?" a voice bellowed loudly enough to shake the bus. Everyone froze.

"Mom?!" I screeched, realizing for the first time that tears were in my eyes.

My mother moved forward quickly past me.

"Go get in the car," she said as she passed. Ngozi and I quickly obeyed.

I never saw how my mother diffused the situation, but for the next month she waited for us at the bus stop to make sure all was well. And for a while, we didn't have to run as much.

This incident must have surprised my mother a bit. We didn't complain to our parents about the kids from school or the neighborhood. Once again, we assumed that dealing with such things was part of the territory, part of being who we were, where we were. Our parents had raised us well, and for that reason we didn't walk with hunched shoulders or feel ashamed of our dark skin, our names, or anything else that made us girls of African descent. Still, our mother had a sixth sense. And that day, she appeared.

But a mother cannot always patrol the world of a child. The minute she stopped waiting at the bus stop, the harassment recommenced. And now, as the three of us stood at that dead end, facing the enemy, it was the moment of truth. I balled up a fist.

"Where're you monkeys gonna run now?!" Michelle Ryan sang. The rest of the kids grinned uneasily. They had never caught their prey and they weren't sure what to do. But I saw their hands, clenched and shaking. And I saw the look in their eyes that broadcast group violence. This was not a good situation. We were significantly outnumbered and outweighed. Most of them were older than we were, and most of them were boys. We had only a moment to decide what to do. There was a tall, leggy blond boy to the left.

We hadn't been raised to give up. Our parents had come to the United States with little and had made much. They knew of the racism that would attempt to hold them back, and they maneuvered their way around it. Where there was a will, there was a way. In this case, a way out.

The three of us acted at the same time. I moved forward, and my sisters moved backward. I lunged and dove, right through the blond boy's legs, jumped to my feet, and took off. Behind me, Ngozi and Ifeoma easily scaled the fence and were gone. The group stood, indecisive about whom to chase, and then instantly gave up.

I ran and ran. Past houses, empty lots, cars, and driveways. Rounded the corner and ran some more. As fast as my legs would take me. And when I got home, I threw the door open and ran inside.

Neon Scars

Wendy Rose

I hate it when other people write about my alienation and anger. Even if it's true, I'm not proud of it. It has crippled me, made me sick, made me out of balance. It has also been the source of my poetry.

Writing this autobiographical essay has been the most difficult, most elusive task I have faced as a writer. I work hard to be less self-involved, less self-centered, less self-pitying. As readers and listeners have noted the angry or somber tone of my poems, I have struggled to lessen these things or, at least, keep them in proportion. I work toward balance and attempt to celebrate at least as often as I moan and rage. Everything I have ever written is fundamentally autobiographical, no matter what the topic or style; to state my life now in an orderly way with clear language is actually to restate, simplified, what has already been said. If I could just come right out and state it like that, as a matter of fact, I would not have needed the poetry. If I could look my childhood in the eye and describe it, I would not have needed to veil those memories in metaphor. If I had grown up with a comfortable identity, I would not need to explain myself from one or another persona. Poetry is both ultimate fact and ultimate fiction; nothing is more brutally honest and, at the same time, more thickly coded.

When I speak of bruises that rise on my flesh like blue marbles, do you understand that these are real bruises that have appeared on my flesh? Or has the metaphor succeeded in hiding the pain while producing the fact, putting it in a private place just for those readers and listeners who know me well enough to have seen the bruises? I live with ghosts and, like anyone who lives with ghosts, I am trapped inside their circle. I long for someone to siphon off the pain, someone to tell it all to, someone to be amazed at how well I have survived. There is both a need for and a revulsion from pity. More than pity, I have needed respect. More than respect, I have needed to be claimed by someone as their own, someone who is wanted. I have survived—and there is pride in that fact—but is my survival of any value? Is my survival different from the millions of survivals in the world? Or is its kinship with them the truth of the matter—that we are growing, reproducing, living together as relations? Is my survival the final proof I have needed that I belong here after all? Will I be missed someday?

When I was first approached for this essay, my response (which lasted for several months) was simply to insist that the editor take some body of my poetic work and let it speak for me. I must have decided that there is some reason to make my pain public, although I am enough of a coward to keep the greatest pain (and the greatest pleasure) to myself. Would releasing the secrets let loose a passion so great and so uncontrolled that it would destroy the poetry? I am told that I take risks. When I am told that, the tellers mean that I take risks artistically, in style or technique, in placing the words on the page just so in a way that other poets would have the sense or the training not to do. It is usually meant as a compliment.

Do you know what is the greatest risk of all? Someday I may be forced to see myself as in a sweat vision, wide open to the world. I may find that I am only that one I saw in the vision, no more, no less. I am only what you see. The vision is naked and cannot be tampered with. Is it enough? Will the voices that have always said I am not good enough be quiet? Is this worth the pain and the poetry? Will you be satisfied?

Facts: May 7, 1948. Oakland. Catholic hospital. Midwife nun, no doctor. Citation won the Kentucky Derby. Israel was born. The United Nations met for the first time. It was Saturday, the end of the baby boom or the beginning. Boom. Stephen's little sister. Daughter of Betty. Almost named Bodega, named Bronwen instead. Little brown baby with a tuft of black hair. Baptized in the arms of Mary and Joe. Nearly blind for ten years. Glasses. Catholic school. Nuns with black habits to their ankles. Heads encased in white granite. Rosary beads like hard apricots—measuring prayers, whipping wrists. Paced before the blackboard. Swore in Gaelic. Alone. Alone at home. Alone in the play yard. Alone at Mass. Alone on the street. Fed, clothed in World War II dresses, little more. Mom too sick to care; brother raised by grandparents. Alone. Unwatched. Something wrong with me; everyone knows but me. They all leave me alone. No friends. Confirmation. Patron Francis of Assisi. He understands. Public high school. Drugs, dropping out. Finally friends. Getting high, staying high. Very sick, hospital. No more drugs, no more friends. Alone again. Married at eighteen. Tried to shoot me. Lasted three months. Again at nineteen. Lived in basement, then in trailer. Worked in Yosemite. Sold Indian crafts. Went on display. Drinking, fighting, he tried to burn down the house; he gave me the name Rose. Starved in Nevada; nearly died. Home. Eating again; got fat. College. Graduated in ten years. Went to grad school. Alone again. Met Arthur. Fell in love, still happy. Another ten years. Live in a nice house. Fresno. Have a swimming pool. Air conditioning. Have an old cat. Rent a typewriter. Teach. Work on doctorate. Two of us now. Moved to another planet, home.

Healing.

I am probably my mother. She bears my face but is lighter in complexion, taller, long-legged. She was thin enough as a girl to have been teased for it. Her eyebrows each come to a point in the center, little tepees at the top of her face. My brother inherited these, while I got her upward-turned nose and hair that thins at the temple. From my father I have coarse dark hair, a flatness of face and mouth, no waist, a body made of bricks. At different times, I have resembled each of them. I see myself in old photographs of my mother as a short, stocky, dark version of her, and others have seen my father in me, thinner, younger, lighter, female.

As much as I have come from them, the two of them threw me away. I am the part of them that they worked long and hard to cut off. I have never depended on them. I have floated into the distance, alone.

I have heard Indians joke about those who act as if they had no relatives. I wince, because I have no relatives. They live, but they threw me away—so I do not have them. I am without relations. I have always swung back and forth between alienation and relatedness. As a child, I would run away from the beatings, from the obscene words, and always knew that if I could run far enough, then any leaf, any insect, any bird, any breeze could bring me to my true home. I knew I did not belong among people. Whatever they hated about me was a human thing; the nonhuman world has always loved me. I can't remember when it was otherwise. But I have been emotionally crippled by this. There is nothing romantic about being young and angry, or even about turning that anger into art. I go through the motions of living in society, but never feel a part of it. When my family threw me away, every human on earth did likewise.

I have been alone too much. I have been bitter too long. This part of me is not in balance. It has made me alien. This is something to pray about.

There is only one recent immigrant in my family. Sidney, my mother's father, came from England around the turn of the 20th century. I don't know his father's name, but his mother was Christine. Early pictures of Sidney show a serious English schoolboy intent on his economic future. What he did in America was learn photography and operate a small studio in Berkeley for the rest of his life. He took misty portraits of young girls and babies, Victorian still-lifes, and sweeping panoramas of San Francisco Bay.

I don't remember being touched by Sidney at all, but he was my brother's greatest influence. Even today, there is a British clip to my brother's speech. When I was in his house, Sidney was always on the other side of some door. I have wondered, too, why his middle name was "Valdez." And how he came to be so dark and brooding as a young man, so gray when old. Why did he leave England? Where did he meet Clare, the mountain girl from Mariposa, who would give birth to my mother?

Clare was born thirty years after the Gold Rush, in Bear Valley. Bear Creek branches from the Merced River near there, just down the mountain from Yosemite, rippling through oak-wooded, grassy hills and bull-pines. Her mother and father were born there also; he was raised in a house that had belonged to John C. Fremont. Their people had ridden wagons west across the plains or had sailed around the Horn to find prosperity in a land newly claimed from Mexico. Clare's father, Maurice, was the son of German immigrants who had traveled from Missouri in a wagon train; there is a story told by his mother, Margaret, of how one night Indians came to steal the babies. Clare's mother, Elizabeth, had a noble and well-documented lineage. Her people were known by name all the way back to the eighth century on the Scottish side and to the Crusades on the Irish. The dominant thread in her ancestry crossed into Britain with William the Conqueror, part of the family rumored to have been related to him through one of his brothers. The Normans of my mother's background are very well documented and include the modern Lord Dunboyne, although our branch of the Dunboynes split from his during the seventeenth century. This Norman part of the family included Butlers and Massys, Barretts and Percys, Le Petits and de Berminghams—names that fiercely colonized Ireland and settled on stolen land. Among the parts of Ireland that they stole were certain women: O'Brien of Thomond, McCarthy Reagh, Carthach of Muskerry, all representing royal native Irish families. Another thread can be followed to the Scottish Highlands and to royal Celtic and Pictish families via the clans MacInnes and Drummond.

By the time Clare was born in the 1880s, the family had included an Indian man, most probably Miwok. Clare's blonde hair and transparently blue eyes belied that less well-known (and possibly involuntary) heritage, but the native blood reappeared in my mother. How many almost-comic photographs do I have of the sharp-faced blonde and delicate lady who sits before the long-faced mustached Englishman and, between them, holds the chubby little girl with the dark round face, that little Indian baby?

Late in the summer of 1984, I received a package from my mother's cousin Joe, who is also my godfather, although I had not seen him for more than thirty years. He was both black sheep and bachelor in the family, a mystery man of whom I have no clear memories. Now I am laughing at myself. I have always searched for my place and my people, focusing that search on my father. His Hopi people have been sympathetic but silent; they trace their lineage through the mother, and I could never be more than the daughter of a Hopi man. How ironic and unexpected Joe's package was! It contained diary excerpts, lists of names and dates, and newspaper clippings about my mother's family. She had always refused to answer questions about ancestry, citing the melting pot as her excuse. My interest in our heritage was, in her eyes, just an aberration which—like slipping away from the Church—would someday be fixed. Yet the package with its precious communication came to me.

Now why didn't Joe send it to my brother? My brother is what they wanted. He is white-looking, with brown hair and green eyes; he has maintained his ties to home and hearth, even while in the Army. He has expressed great interest in his European blood, has dabbled in Druidic and neo-pagan rites, and looks like them. His hair and beard are long, his clothing covered with mystic symbols. The package did not go to him. I gave him and my mother copies of everything; they were as surprised as I that Joe chose me.

I learned that the Normans who stole Irish land went bankrupt, lost their land, and booked passage in 1830 to Quebec. The MacInnes clan, near that time, was forbidden to wear the tartan and fled Scotland to preserve their heritage.

The weekend after Joe's package arrived, Highland Games were held in Fresno. In no other year would it have occurred to me to attend, but Arthur and I walked onto the grounds to search for my roots, he Japanese and I wearing all my turquoise for courage. It may have looked funny to all those Scots to see an Indian looking for a booth with her clan's name on it. The first booth was Irish; I showed my list of ancestral names to the man there, and he pointed to certain ones and said they had stolen his castle. I apologized to all of Ireland on behalf of John Bull and returned his castle to him; I suspect it would not hold up in Parliament and, anyway, they were the ancestors who had gone bankrupt. This is not the heritage I would have picked—to be the daughter of the invaders. It is not where my sympathies lie. Searching the grounds, I found my clan.

Great-great-grandmother, Henrietta MacInnes, who came to California for gold from Quebec, you have given me what my own father could not. I learned that I am entitled to wear your tartan, your symbol of a strong arm pointing to the sky with a bow in its hand. I also learned that you were the natives of Scotland, descended from the Pictish king, Onnus, and lent strength to my apology for Ireland. The colonizer and the colonized meet in my blood. It is so much more complex than just white and just Indian. I will pray about this, too.

This year, Sidney and Clare, Grandad and Nana, are turning real for me. They have been dead twenty-five years, but my thoughts go to them as I continue to listen to my mother's jokes about their embarrassment. Clare got so angry sometimes! Like when people would ask what racial mixture her little girl, my mother, was. Or when that little girl shared a room with a Jew in college. Or when that little girl, who had bobbed her hair and hung out with flappers, married a man with Indian blood and rural background. Clare knew who to blame. My mother told me of her mother's peculiar habit of taking my brother into her home when he was sick to nurse him back to health and, when I was sick, of taking my brother into her home so he wouldn't catch what I had. She was amused by this.

Nana! I'm afraid you'll see me cry! I have never been able to cry in front of you, of anyone. Any strong emotion is dangerous, as people are dangerous. Poetry has been the safest way to cry in public. I bristle when people say I'm cold and unfriendly, but they're right. I can't tell you straight out how I feel without putting it into a poem. And I have written some for you, safely cloaked in metaphor or masked by a persona. I hope you understand that the poetry is the only way I can love you. I *do* love. But you are dangerous. Does Mom know how much it hurts when she tells me about the way you turned from me? Does she know how much it hurts for me to know that it could have gone unsaid?

I am turning numb. I have been educated to put a name to the things that my parents did, but the child within has no such knowledge. I recall that every dirty word I ever knew was first heard from my father's lips, from the man who raised me as he struck over and over. As an adult, I take this apart and study it. I suppose it was a kind of rape for him to talk like that in the middle of his violence, to name the parts of my body he intended to mutilate or cut away. I recall lying in my bed, hearing him scream at my mother that he wanted to kill me; and I recall that he tried, more than once. Symbolic of what he wanted to do to me, he smashed my toys. My mother's memories float in and out of those scenes; at times she denies everything, but I remember it was she who pulled him away as he tried to choke me on my bed. There was no media hype about abuse in those days, no public awareness; I begged the police to put me in a foster home, but I was always sent back. Eventually I learned that I was to blame for all of this, just as I was to blame for my parents' unhappiness.

I embarrassed them. They tell me their marriage began to go bad when I was born, although they never divorced. He lives in one room, she in another. How much it must embarrass them now for me to say these things to strangers! I would say something else, be someone else, act some other way—but there is no way I can twist my genes around. There is no sugar sweet enough to smear on the story of our household. These are ghosts that will never leave, the ghosts of knowing how I destroyed their lives. They sent me to social workers and psychiatrists, to priests, to people whose roles or professions I never knew. They told me I was sick and must try to get better so that my family could mend. Everything, they said, depended on me. I just wanted to get out so that the beatings, the obscene language about my body, and the constant knowledge of his hatred would be far away. Didn't they believe what I told them? Couldn't they see the scars? I didn't know that such scars never heal up. It's probably lucky that my nature is a fighting one; otherwise I would have died.

I will talk about being different, as if I were talking about someone else. My mother said I was born different.

Her mother said she was born different. No one ever said what that difference was all about, but everyone knew it when they saw it. They avoided it as if it burned them. And so she was always alone and not just alone, but thrown away. They made sure she knew she was being thrown away. They told her so, over and over, through action and word, until she could see it no other way. And so she knew she was rejected and she knew she was rejectable. She learned to worship her difference, whatever it was, and this empowered her. She rejected them.

Or, I could try this. I'll make up a story about my childhood and see if anyone believes it. I will tell about happy summer days with all my friends. Us girls are trying on makeup, combing each other's hair, comparing lies about boyfriends. The boys all want to date me, but I can only choose one at a time. I hate to hurt the others. I have been riding my beautiful stallion on the mountain; alongside is my healthy young collie. I know that when I go home, my parents will be glad to see me; they'll hug me and kiss me and hold me. Uncles and aunts and cousins will be there, too, and they will hug me. They know all about me, what my interests are, what I did that day. I have been placed in the gifted program at school and will be high school valedictorian. I have been skipping grades because everyone thinks I'm so smart. I'm pretty, too. I will enter college at seventeen with an enormous scholarship. I will receive gold jewelry or a diamond for my graduation. My father will kiss me on the cheek and take my picture.

I don't want to lie to you, but I don't want to tell the truth. The dirty laundry flaps in the wind, yet the alternative is to go on wearing it. How do you admit in public that you were abused, that the only time your parents ever touched you— that you can remember—was in anger, that your cousins probably don't know you exist, that your own grandparents had no use for you? How do you acknowledge that you were left so alone you never learned to brush your teeth or fix your food? How do you reveal that you were a bag lady at fourteen, having been turned out of the house, or that when you ran away no one looked for you? How do you expect anyone to believe how hungry you were at times, how you nearly died from starvation twice—when they can plainly see how fat you are now? How do you explain that you dropped out of high school, were classified as retarded but educable, and were not allowed to take college-prep classes? How do you reconcile being an "Indian writer" with such a non-Indian upbringing? It is not the Indian way to be left so alone, to be alienated, to be friendless, to be forced to live on the street like a rat, to be unacquainted with your cousins. It would certainly be better for my image as an Indian poet to manufacture something and let you believe in my traditional, loving, spiritual childhood where every winter evening was spent immersed in storytelling and ceremony, where the actions of every day continually told me I was valued.

Today, I live about fifty miles from Bear Valley. As I write, it is early August and the days are valley-hot, the nights thickly warm and filled with crickets. Although last winter was dry, this summer has found an explosion of toads in my yard. To uncover the memories, I have peeled back layers of scar tissue.

I have invoked the ghosts and made them work for me. Is that the answer? To keep them busy? There is nothing authentic or nice about my past; I am sure that I would be a great disappointment to anthropologists. But then, you know—now— why I write poetry; being Indian was never the reason. I have agonized for months about writing this essay, and now that it is finished I am afraid of it. I am mortified and embarrassed. I am certain I said too much, whined perhaps, made someone squirm. But there is no way I can change the past, and the literal fact is that I have tried to forget what is unforgettable; there are few happy moments that I recall—or perhaps, as I have succeeded in forgetting the bad, the good has also been forgotten. Perhaps the editor and the readers will forgive me for using them in an exorcism.

My father told me, when I took Arthur down to Hopi to meet him, that Hopi earth does contain my roots and I am, indeed, from that land. Because the roots are there, I will find them. But when I find them, he said, I must rebuild myself as a Hopi. I am not merely a conduit, but a participant. I am not a victim, but a woman.

I am building myself.
There are many roots.
I plant, I pick, I prune.
I consume.

Betsy, Tacy, Sejal, Tib

Sejal Shah

In the books I read growing up, there were always words I couldn't quite imagine. I remember, with a specificity that surprises me, the foreignness of certain colors: *kelly green, strawberry blonde.* These were books about girls with doting fathers and best friends named George, books about an adopted boy named Jim and his sister, Honey. A series about two best friends from the same street who made room for a third. No one felt alone past the second chapter. A series about twins, one good and one slightly more interesting. Like every girl, I wanted a twin or a best friend. Like every girl, I wanted both. Another series: four girls away at camp—it was in truth a boarding school, but I could scarcely imagine such a thing. That's what I mouthed to myself, then: scarcely. I tried these words on in my head, alone in my room, the bedside lamp on, folded under the covers, escaping into the pages of a book. And isn't that what all writers want? Falling into a book, each one a kind of Narnia, and feeling that exquisite edge of aloneness, honed almost to happiness.

Nearly everything that happened in my life when I was twelve took place at home, or at some close distance from home. My mother would say to me, "Will you get the matching blouse from my drawer? It's *popti*-colored. Parrot green." In my head, this was the same color as kelly green, but I never found out. I never knew for sure. There were certain colors that bloomed normal on the palette of Indian saris, hanging in rows in the guest bedroom/youngest daughter's closet. The way I'd seen in all of my friends' houses, too—the saris couldn't fit into the parents' closets. Saris and American clothes would not coexist in the same shallow closet of these first houses.

How these series come back to haunt me now, with their sense of ownership over the world, with the ways in which they defined a world. *Kelly green.* With all the ways in which they owned words. *Strawberry blonde.* We read these books, but there was no one like us in any of them. Did we think of writing our own? I want to see us. To see the girl I was, the girls we were, back when we lived at home.

Something like Nancy Drew: *The Secret of the Old Clock, The Clue of the Leaning Chimney. The Mystery of the Girl Who Lives at Home.*

Sejal Shah lived alone with her parents on Pelham Road in western New York State, in a city that had seen better days ("Lion of the West"), that had housed stops on the Underground Railroad. She became a late only child, her older brother having jumped ship for college, Brown University, where many of the students were colored, mixed

race, radical, or in some other way Third World, yet wanting to begin their training to be doctors, investment
bankers, nonprofit organizers, painters, members of the
educated elite. Sejal, when not solving mysteries ("The Case
of the Unfinished Homework") or staying away from those
less fortunate and more maligned than herself (resource
room kids, kids born in India who now faced the horrors of
gym class and enforced classroom pairing), spent her days
in the company of Esprit-wearing white kids (Jessica, Tara,
Amity, Kathleen), trying to avoid the ball in volleyball, running fast in track. They were incredulous over the obvious:
Three others in town shared her first name, two of whom
shared both her names. It was necessary to use middle ini-
tials so as not to confuse the library system and the eye doctor's office: Sejal A., Sejal B., Sejal N. Shah (there was no C.).
On the weekend, Sejal A. was joined by her trio of friends.
They were all girls with glasses: Sonal, Mini, and Rupali. As
you might expect, there were also two boys: Nitin and
Manish. Nicky and Max. Even their parents called them by
these names, the nicknames an improvement for their junior
high lives. Their secret Indian lives—this is what bound
them, the Secret Six, together.

During the week, they tried to look like everyone else.
On the weekends, they stopped trying. On the weekends,
they headed to each other's houses. The girls took turns
hosting sleepovers, figuring out which boy they liked. All
of them parodied their parents' accents; then they repeated
the joke about how their parents ordered a cheeseburger

without the burger at McDonalds and asked to talk to the manager, Ronald McDonald, when they were not understood; then they taught each other how to use curling irons to fix their bangs without accidentally making awkward cowlick angles. In each other's kitchens, they ate Hot Mix (Rice Krispies, potato sticks, peanuts, lemon juice, and murchu); practiced moonwalking; kept secret track of who got her period first, watched their mothers making chaa and finding the crushed red pepper to sprinkle on pizza, and their fathers debating something or playing carom. In each other's bedrooms and bathrooms, the girls experimented with hair-removal systems—that noxious cream, Nair, which only sometimes worked, and hydrogen peroxide (sure, some Indians have blonde hair, Sejal tried to tell her brother). In each other's bedrooms, Sejal and Mini gingerly tried out Sally Hansen Natural Cold Wax Kit for Face/Leg/Body/Bikini. Sonal and Sejal tried hot wax with cloth strips and gave themselves minor burns across their legs. Their sensible mothers had warned them about how using a razor would only mean the hair would grow back thicker. Finally, the girls gave up and found the plastic bag of Bic disposable razors one of their fathers used. Then it was time to find Band-Aids and introduce the real topic of conversation: tampons—just how exactly did that work?

In each other's houses, they could relax. No explanations were necessary about why their mothers did or did not wear saris, about what that dot meant (how were they supposed to know?), about the difference between Hindu and

Hindi, about why their parents were stricter than American parents, about why they always took their shoes off in the house. They were four girls and two boys. They could have fit neatly into a book.

Boy #1 was the nice one. Boy #2 played the drums. Girl #1 went to school west of the city. She was the only Indian in her school, no small cross to bear in the early '80s. Sonal's mother, Nalini Auntie, was best friends with Sejal's mother, Shobhana Auntie. Girl #2 went to Catholic school—a whole different world from the other girls' schools. Mini wore a uniform, and her school had dress-down days. She and her sister were also the only Indians there. Girl #3 lent Sejal her dress for the eighth-grade formal ("A Night in Paris"). It was a silky gray dress with puffed sleeves. Without Rupali's help, Sejal might have been forced to wear a dress her mother liked. Sejal's mother often said, "School is not a fashion parade!" and Sejal, Sonal, Rupali, and Mini would laugh, because all of their parents said it. And *of course* school was a fashion parade. The girls had to know what to wear—this mattered even more if you looked different. Rupali's father, Sumant Uncle, always drove the kids to the multiplex. The girls watched their little sisters and stayed at the movies for hours, slipping from one theater to another, thrilling at seeing even the last fifteen minutes of a movie they didn't like, just to stay a little longer.

Three of the four girls had at least one parent who had grown up in Africa. Sejal wondered if her own parents and her friends' parents somehow felt more comfortable with each other than with other Indians. They, like the girls, had grown up outside of India. They had to approximate India, too. They were play-acting, too: outdated gestures, films, food. Some of them must have read the Famous Five books by Enid Blyton, a British series, but all of the kids in that series were white. Sejal and her brother read comic books: Archie, Veronica, and Betty right next to stacks of Amar Chitra Katha books. Arjuna's dilemma over whether or not to fight his cousins on the battlefield held their interest as much as Archie's never-ending struggle between Betty and Veronica. It was a tough choice: Betty was blonde, but Veronica was rich.

I remember us, think back to us, to the dilemmas of any middle-school girl: the mysteries of the notes we wrote each other. Four girls, and someone was always the odd one out. Of the strategies we deployed to catch the boys' attention: HCP = hard, cold, polite. Alternating with F+F: friendly and flirtatious. Those were the only strategies we had. We also tried to learn how to throw a football, how to hit a baseball, how to play pool, how to swim. Who had the words to talk about that other mystery: how to be American, how not to be American?

I wonder if the other girls felt the way I did. That we needed a series portraying fathers who said no dating till college (or ever), with characters eating *pani puri* and *prasaad*, emptying out dresser drawers for the cousin who had come to stay for three months or two years. Did they also wonder when peacock blue, henna red, and *popti* green would appear in those books? When the names Shalini, Neelu, Ajay, and Sunil would appear? There would be no need to describe the color of the characters' hair: All of them would have black hair, maybe with brown highlights as they got older. And maybe I would have to remember to mention the green and blue and hazel contact lenses the girls began to wear as they got older. I see them still, see all of us still, wearing our glasses. How awkward and beautiful we were, in our fake Izods, in our Sears. How mysterious and cruel we were, how kind and belly-laughable.

I wanted them all: pulp paperbacks, spines broken, or hardbacks in plastic jackets, the slip of paper on the inside page with all of the library stamps: date after date after date. The covers of the older series were painted the brown and red of the late 1970s. Muted colors—olive; that weathered Margaret Thatcher blue-gray; lilac-heather on the hardbacks of *Anne of Green Gables*. It is how I think of those summer evenings, those Sunday afternoons. The days Sonal and I used brown paper grocery bags to bring back a stack of books from either of our town libraries. How we stretched out in her room on Avocado Lane, reading, before roller-skating down the driveway, before it was time to set the table for dinner.

The Gujarati Girls Go to (Hindu Heritage Summer) Camp, The Gujarati Girls Go Skiing, The Mystery of the Prasaad Plate (A Gujarati Girls Mystery), *The Gujarati Girls Go to Panorama Plaza* (to see the latest Molly Ringwald movie—Gujarati Girls Mystery #13), *The Gujarati Girls Get Malaria* (also titled *The Gujarati Girls Go to India).*

My friends now laugh (it seems almost like a novel) at the stories about how I grew up, how we grew up. We took cup baths, never used the dishwasher except as a drying rack, saved tin foil, almost never ate out. Is that world gone? We were more Indian once, I know this. We were something else once. I feel this as a nearly physical ache, this knowledge, because it means I am something else now.

Still, I am telling you this story, I am telling me this story as a way to remember how we laughed, how we read, how we knew *our* friendships were different. How we knew our lives were more interesting than Nancy Drew's. I don't know if I was the only one who wanted to see our faces in what we read, to see our split-level houses, our CorningWare dishes and Duralex glasses, our fake wood coffee tables with their stacks of *Time* and *Reader's Digest* (not a *New Yorker* anywhere)— our particular blend of suburban Rochester and middle-class Gujarati—but I am the one who became a writer. I am writing this, on a Wednesday afternoon in Western Massachusetts, thinking ahead to when I will see them, my Gujarati girls, next. Wondering if those books, were I to see them now—if they would mean the same thing to me. Betsy, Tacy, and Tib. Trixie Belden. The Girls of Canby Hall. Anne of Green Gables. Nancy Drew. Sweet Valley High. How could they?

The Gujarati Girls Grow Up

Sejal Shah, Manisha Patel, Sonal Dubey, and Rupali Grady were headed to another wedding. "Don't worry," Sejal said confidently, "I see the way over here to the left." And she led the way to the door and opened it.

As American as Apple Pie

B. Lois Wadas

Gamma is arranging the pie-making stuff in the dining room. She has spoons and all kinds of pans and bowls on the dining room table. It is the spring of 1956. I am on Easter break from school.

They killed my daddy.

Gamma is talking to herself again. I'm not really listening. She always does that when she's working. I'm watching her hands. Her knuckles are big and knobby. Her fingers are crooked from hard work. Sometimes her fingers swell. She says it's Mr. Arthur Ritis. I have to say "Mister" because children can't call grownups by their first name. I wonder if her hands hurt. I hope Mr. Arthur Ritis never gets in my fingers. She has wire curlers in her hair, the kind with the plastic pins to hold them in place. How does she sleep on those things?

"Gal, give me that bowl," she says, and then, without even looking at me, "No, not that one." She doesn't want the blue cereal bowl I offer. She points with her elbow. I go get the big yellow bowl, the one with the flowers around the rim. It's in the drain tray in the sink. I look out our kitchen window, which overlooks the project playground. I scan the yard below. Tyrone and Kay are playing skellies out there, with tar-filled bottle caps on a chalked-up sidewalk.

It's Saturday. Tomorrow is Easter Sunday. Gamma and I are making apple pie. My mother and brothers are out shopping for Easter clothes. Miss Margaret is braiding my little sisters' hair. I have my Easter outfit already. I will be pretty at church. Gamma says people who don't go to church are heathens. I don't know what that means, but I don't want to be one. Today, we make pie for tomorrow's dessert.

They said the house wasn't ours, but it was our house. His daddy sharecropped that land and he give it and the house to my daddy when he married my momma. He had the papers and everything.

Gamma sounds mad. She always sounds mad when she gets to the part about the house. I used to think she was mad at me. Now, I don't really even listen. She's just talking.

Some other boys join Tyrone and Kay playing skellies. The sun has rendered their skin an ebony shine. "Hey, big head!" I yell, and then duck behind the curtains.

When I peek around the edge of the window shade, I can see Tyrone looking up at the building. He squints, and then uses one dirty hand to shield his eyes. "Yo momma!" he yells in the direction of my voice. I giggle and jerk back so he can't see me.

"Gal! Stop playing and gimme that bowl." Gamma is half turned toward me. She has one flour-dusted hand on her hip.

Her eyes are tight, and her mouth is pouty. I bring the bowl, careful to hold it with two hands. I watch her mouth. Her bottom lip is poked out like a shelf. I want to laugh, but I don't. Gamma is very serious about cooking.

She says I have to learn to cook and bake if I want to feed my husband. She always says that about housework. I'm only nine and I don't want a husband. I just want to eat warm apple pie.

I put my cookbook on the table and open to the page I have marked for making apple pie. "Child," Gamma sighs, "your schoolbooks don't belong in the kitchen." "It's not a schoolbook, Gamma." I show her the book's cover. "It's a cookbook," I say as I clear a space for it on the counter.

"Books don't belong in the kitchen," she says under her breath. Gamma can't read.

I think that she can read a little bit though, because she went to school in That Forsyth Georgia. Gamma always says "that" Forsyth Georgia. So I say it the way she does. Momma told me that Gamma only went to the third grade. She said when Gamma was a girl, colored people didn't go to school the way we do today.

I read the ingredients for our pie. I run my finger down the page to make sure Gamma didn't forget anything.

He was going to the courthouse to show them the papers in his name. He couldn't read but he could sign his name. My momma could read. Her daddy was a preacher. Not no jackleg preacher either. Her daddy was a real preacher. She and her daddy both could read. She read him the deed papers and told him to take them down to the courthouse. I 'member the day they went down there to file those papers. They got dressed up and walked all the way to town. He had on his white shirt Sister ironed for him. Momma wore her Sunday hat. It was hot out that day . . .

Gamma is checking the oven and work-talking at the same time. "Gamma, we don't have any lemon juice." I am running my finger down the recipe page. "What?" she asks from inside the oven. Then she straightens up and looks at me. "We don't have any lemon juice." I say it again. Sometimes Gamma doesn't listen.

"What we need lemon juice for?" she asks. Now her lip is really poked out. I bet those wire curlers are hot.

"The recipe says lemon juice." I stare at her curlers. Gamma frowns and tucks in her lip.

"Lemon juice in apple pie?" She says it like I said "tuna fish" in apple pie. I don't say anything. I just point to the page. "Book cooking ain't real cooking." She closes the oven door on her way back to the table. She is shaking her head; there is almost a smile in her voice. "Come," she says. I follow her to the table and stand close to her, almost under her arm. Her arm is warm and plump and soft. "When I was a little girl, I used to help my mother cook. I learned by watching and handing her things. We didn't have no book food. So I don't

know nothing about food on a page. I know food on a plate."
She is really talking to me this time.

I feel warm all over and it's not from the hot oven. We forget about lemons and lemon juice. Gamma is not talking now.

We are working together at the dining room table, the one my mother bought when she had some extra money. Momma is proud of her dining room furniture. She keeps polishing the table and moving the chairs around. Gamma and me are making a mess. Momma won't fuss, though, because Gamma will clean it up. Gamma says, "You have to clean as you go."

I am her favorite grandchild, and I know it. She says she does not have a favorite. But I know different.

My momma had to leave walking with sixteen head of children. The big ones carried the little ones. I weren't but six or so. So I only had to carry myself. We walked from That Forsyth Georgia all the way to Macon. We carried what we could, and dragged the rest. We walked away from That Forsyth Georgia. We walked all the way to Macon.

We passed other colored folks walking or standing staring at they houses burning. Most of 'em we passed was women with children. Some looked witless. They lost they wits along with they husband and they house. Most of the houses weren't nothing more than shacks. Ours was a real house, so they didn't burn it. They just took it, along with the grass and trees . . .

Seems like they took the light out the day. I thought daylight would never come.

We lost a daddy to them folks. Some folks lost they whole self, family, and all, from little to big. How could they do it? What they made of?

Gamma is mauling the dough. I want to play with it, too. "Can I do some?" She doesn't answer but moves aside so I can get to the table. There is flour in her hair and on her forehead. She didn't take all the rollers out of her hair. So part of her hair is wired and part is loose.

Gamma has on old-man slippers, but she has crushed the backs down. Her heels are hanging off. Her ankles are swollen. I think of donuts. I kiss her floured cheek. She wipes it off.

The dough ball looks rough. I want to smooth it out. Gamma stops me. "It will be too tight if you do that."

I plunge my hands all spread out into the pasty gray dough and squish it between my fingers. Gamma is standing there watching me. "No baby, ball it up," she says. My heart spreads out. I like us here like this, alone, close and busy. I have her all to myself.

Gamma is quiet. Except for a sigh every now and then, she is quiet. I hope she didn't go back to *That* Forsyth Georgia. I want her to stay here with me. I think *That* Forsyth Georgia is a nasty place.

They wanted a white county is what they said. Momma and Daddy came back from the courthouse and said it was burned down. They said there wasn't no papers to git.

Momma said it was her fault for telling Daddy to put the house papers in there, but Daddy said it wasn't her fault. He said they had their mind set on doing him out of his house anyway they could.

She has gone back to That Forsyth Georgia again.

I bunch the dough, ball it up the way I saw her do it. I look up at her to see if I am doing it right. Gamma is staring at my hands, but she's not looking at me. Her eyes are looking nowhere.

They came in the night. Two big white men with faces like fists. There were two more of them in that old pickup truck they was driving. My daddy opened the door and asked them to come in and set a while. But they wouldn't, said they didn't want to disturb us, said it would be better if he came out with them. Momma didn't want him to go. Just the week before, they took they white hands and killed a boy. So Momma was scared. Her eyes was nervous-looking. She musta knowed he wasn't coming back. He musta knowed, too, 'cause he kissed each and every one of us, even the ones too big for kissin', 'fore he left. He never did that before. He held Momma, too, held her a long time before he went through the door wit them devils. And Momma commenced to crying as soon as that door closed. He musta knowed if he didn't come out, they woulda come in for one and all, and none of us would be here today.

My momma was a woman full of tears, she was. I never knowed a body could cry for so long, seem like to me she never really did stop, not even when I took care of her in her old age, all the time her eyes rolled tears. Even when she wasn't hard crying, her eyes rolled tears, soft crying.

Soon as my daddy went through that door with them devils, Momma sent us, big and little, to bed even though our supper was still on the table, 'tole us to go to sleep. I have always felt shame for thinking about my dinner on that table, all the while my daddy was being killed and my momma cried, "Never stop tears." You'd think God would take appetite and hunger pangs away when your daddy is out being killed. I never did forgive my stomach for that. Anyhow, who could sleep with they momma crying her soul loose in the next room and they daddy out in the woods wit white mens wit the "killing look."

We don't have all the things the recipe is asking for, so I use one of the big glasses to flatten out the pie dough. Gamma showed me how to do this part before. See, all you have to do if you don't have a rolling pin is put some flour on a glass, not too much, then put it on the middle of the dough ball and press and roll in all directions. I'm doing it right.

Gamma takes the glass from me and finishes spreading out the dough. She makes two nice circles. We do have pie pans. Gamma's hands are like magic. She flips each circle of dough right into the pan in one whole piece. Then she uses a fork around the edges. Halfway around, she hands me the fork so I can finish it.

They said it was a car accident. It weren't no car accident. There wasn't a dent in that old truck of theirs. They had him in the back of that old pickup like he was lumber or something. My daddy didn't have a mark on him. His neck was broke though. They broke his neck.

Gamma is work-talking, so I eat some of the apple filling right out the bowl. I even add some more cinnamon. Gamma doesn't notice, because she's back in That Forsyth Georgia.

He never shoulda gone with them. We was all up watching him go through the door. He kissed each of us 'fore he left. Then he was gone. My momma start to crying soon as she closed the door behind him. She musta knowed he wasn't coming back, musta felt it.

We laid him out on the table and washed him down. Then my brothers put his Sunday suit on him. He always looked nice in that suit.

She pauses. Her voice is a whisper.

Handsome.

She says "handsome" like it's a secret.

Gamma slides the pie into the oven. She holds her lower back when she straightens up. I use the sponge to wipe down the table. Gamma starts washing the dishes. I dry.

Later, while Gamma sits on the sofa, I take the rest of the wire curlers out of her hair. She is dozing. Slowly, her head nods. In mid-nod, she catches herself, looks up at me and says,

"My daddy, Robert Hollis, really was handsome you know."
She is really talking to me again, for real.

It's eleven o'clock at night, in the opulent '80s; I am settled on
the side of my bed watching the late news on television. The
commentator is speaking about the NAACP being denied a
parade permit for a protest rally in some town in Georgia. I
am parting my hair and putting sponge curlers into the sections I have just separated. I am only half watching the news.
I'm really trying to distract myself from this nightly chore. My
hair will be wild in the morning if I don't roll it tonight.

The television screen provides only flickering light in the
room. I have put my house to bed hours ago. All the doors are
locked. The trash is out and the kitchen is clean. There are no
dishes in the sink. My son and daughter have been asleep since
nine o'clock.

I use the remote to mute the television. Whatever is going
on, I don't want to take it into my dreams. I decide not to listen. I am thinking about paying my mortgage and maybe even
refinancing my house. I would like to remodel my kitchen. *My
house.* I smile at the thought. Home ownership is delicious. I
have satisfied my compulsion to own my own piece of the
rock. Now all I need to do is keep it.

We have a "thing" in our family about owning homes and
education. It is a serious thing, too, almost an infection. It

lives a quietly throbbing life. When the cousins get together, the children and grandchildren of the original sixteen Hollises, it's almost an "I'll show you mine if you show me yours" atmosphere. I smile. Okay, I've done it. I have fulfilled the unspoken family dictum. I am a single parent and I own a house! This is no small feat for a black woman by herself. I worked hard to make it happen. It's not much of a house, but I am willing to work hard to keep it.

I only wish my grandmother had lived long enough to see me make it happen. Sometimes I have dreams about her coming back.

In one dream, I go downstairs into my kitchen and she is standing there at the sink. I know she has crossed over. However, I am not afraid. I am concerned, though. "Grandma," I say in the dream, "What's the matter, why aren't you resting?" She turns slowly and says directly to me, "I'm not finished." I understand what she means without her explaining. She walks to the foot of the stairs leading to the bedrooms and bathroom on the second floor. I let her go without following her.

I wait in the kitchen for what seems like a long time. Then I go to find her. She is in the bathroom. The door is closed. I get down on the floor and look under the door. She is dancing, spinning really. Her arms are folded across her chest.

I continue to peek under the door until she spins out. She dissolves. The dream is so real I wake up and walk through the house looking for her.

I really expect to find her in the bathroom. I am grieved that I cannot find her anywhere. I want her to stay with me. I still miss her. Yet, I feel blessed by her visit. She has blessed *our* house.

The television camera pans a crowd of angry white faces. I hit the remote to bring the sound back on. What is going on? My hands pause above my hair, a roller in one hand, and a section of hair in the other. The commentator is saying something about an all-white county. I can feel my insides ball up. Now I am very focused on the television; something, something familiar is hatching in my head. My telephone rings. I look at the clock on my bedside table: 11:20 P.M. Who would be calling me at this time? I pick up the receiver.

It's my cousin. Before she can say more than "Hello," I say, "Margie, there is something on the news about an all-white county in Georgia. I feel like I am supposed to know something about this." She laughs. "Of course you do. That's where they lynched your great-grandfather."

Apple pie, work-talking, broken necks, stolen houses, murdered boys, and children walking in the night flood my memory. An image of my grandmother flashes large and insistent behind my eyes. My heart is racing. I remember! Grandma, I remember!

There will be no sleep for me tonight. I am wide awake and tingling. I am excited and filled with a gentle sorrow. Grandma was telling me her life all those years. She told it the only way she could. She told it to me in bits and pieces. Her life leaked out in unguarded moments of distracted work. She told it when her hurt and sorrow overflowed. She told it against her will. She told it when the tucks and folds of her heart loosed and became unlatched. She gave it to me without burden. She gave it to me to hold for her, to remember for her. She told it in a dazed state, a disconnected remembering, more like a reliving. She was back in That Forsyth Georgia each time she work-talked.

The night comes alive for me, filled with re-memory and my grandmother, Carrie Hollis-Pitts, reliving.

She spoke in her dream state of work-talking, while washing floors or doing laundry. She told me and told me and told me. And her telling went into my psyche, from her to me in bits and pieces.

I drag out her metal box of papers. There are old photos in there, and a death certificate worn and yellow. It is fragile. I handle it carefully; some of the pieces are missing. The death certificate is for John Pitts. He was the man who married her. He was the man from whom she ran away. He died in Alabama; he had children older than she. I can't make out the date. It looks like 1929. There is another death certificate in there for a man named Willie something. It, too, is fragile, frayed, falling apart in my hands. Who is he? Was he my mother's father? His cause of death is listed as "undetermined."

My memory is load and giving. Thirty years, Grandma, but I do remember! I will breathe life into your life.

Breathing Lessons

Randi Gray Kristensen

When I am small, I am the little girl in the Coppertone ad, running away from the small black dog that has my bikini bottom in its teeth and threatens to pull it off. We have the same small body, the same affinity for bikinis, the same wispy blond hair, and the same giggly combination of pleasure and fear in the encounter of body, sun, dog, and exposure. I am the Coppertone girl on a Jamaican beach, living with my Danish father and pale Jamaican mother in a house where darker Jamaicans clean and tend the garden. My father sits me on his lap and reads me Donald Duck cartoons in Danish, and I am in love with the sound and his arms around me; my mother radiates disapproval and unhappiness, except on days when the rain pours down and I strip to shower outside; then we laugh together. My nickname is "the little chatterbox."

One day, I put my shoes on by myself for the first time, and proudly come down the steps to show off. The maid and her friend are sitting on the steps, and when I point out my achievement, they start laughing, and tell me I have them on the wrong feet. I run back up the steps, ashamed. When I am three, I break my leg climbing boxes in the garage. The nurses at the hospital refuse to give me my stuffed bear; I refuse to let them feed me. They give me Jell-O that winds up all over my sheet. They laugh. I come home in a body cast, with an opening in the back that is rough and uneven, and rubs raw the skin at the top of my thigh. Archie, the gardener, carries me in and out of the house. Sometimes his finger touches the open wound, and I scream. He tells me to shut up, and threatens not to carry me. I swallow the pain. Next to black people, I feel stupid, weak. A failure.

My mother goes away when I am three, and I go to stay with her mother, who is dark like the people who clean my father's house. No servants tend her house, and we do not go to the beach. But there are chickens and a dog and a cat. The cat has kittens; Grandma puts them in a paper bag and drowns them in the rain barrel. I can hear them struggling, and start to cry. She shoos me away, and we never speak of it. I am a little afraid of her after that. A year or so later, my mother comes back; I recognize her from a picture Grandma has. We return to the house with the servants and my father.

This morning in yoga class, the instructor offers a closing thought: "Inhale—this is my body. Exhale—this is my home." This gentle meditation undoes me; I have spent the better part of my lifetime looking for "home."

⚜

When I am four, my mother leaves again. This time she takes me with her. It is morning, and Archie is raking in the yard. She tells me we are going for a ride on an airplane. I ask if Daddy is coming with us. No. I ask if I can say goodbye to him. Later. I do not see him again until I am ten (once) and then again when I am fifteen (once). This time we do not go to Grandma's, but to Washington, D.C. It is 1965, and we have trouble finding an apartment. When my mother says no one wants to rent to her because she has a child, I offer to go with her, to prove to them that I am a good girl. We wind up in a studio apartment near my school and her work as a secretary for the federal government. I attend the French International School because it lasts all day; I learn to cross Connecticut Avenue by myself to go home for lunch and after school. At first the teachers won't let me, but my mother is formidable, and they relent. At five, I am learning to take care of myself.

School is taught in French. In the elevator to our apartment, we hear French and Russian and English and Danish and Spanish. I don't know many Americans, except the minister and his wife and kids down the street. They are white, and they often have black children playing at the house. At the park on Columbia Road, there are people who look like

Jamaica, but they sound different. So do the black students at school, who are the children of African diplomats. After a year in school, we discover I am nearsighted, and I get glasses. The first sentence I read by myself is a full-page ad in the Sunday *Washington Post:* "Vacation in the Bahamas."

I am seven, going on eight. Grandma, who is brown like Hershey's milk chocolate sprinkled with cocoa beans, visits us in Washington. Dr. Martin Luther King, Jr., has been assassinated, and my mother is crying at the television. That afternoon, the city burns. Our apartment window frames a slow tornado of black smoke rising into the nearby sky. Grandma stands at the window and declares, "I didn't come to die in this man's country." I have never seen my mother cry before. When I try to comfort her, she shoos me away.

Our next-door neighbor is a secretary at the French Embassy. She is from someplace like Jamaica, called Guadeloupe. She has us over for dinner, and I am proud to be with the adults. I attempt conversation, telling them that my grandmother would like the fatty cut of meat because she calls it "rich meat." Everyone laughs, and I feel like a social success. That night, as she tucks me in to sleep, my mother tells me that some stories we keep in the family, because other people might not understand and might think less of us for them. I am crushed: I have embarrassed my grandmother and disappointed my mother. I don't know how to tell the difference between good stories and bad ones, so I keep them all to myself.

I am nine years old, in boarding school in Jamaica. Like every other school I have gone to, people come in all shades: pale like condensed milk, dark like molasses, and everything in between. This new place frightens me, but I am relieved by the distance from my mother's determination to punish me into a shape I'm having trouble fitting. Spankings seem out of proportion to crimes; I am already torn between the mysteries of pleasing her and the desire to escape. The other girls interrogate me: "Are you color-prejudiced?" I know what color means; I know what prejudiced means; I don't know what they mean together, or why the girls I want to be friends with stare at me so intently while they wait for my answer. "Yes," I declare bravely. "My favorite color is green." They laugh and the moment passes. But slowly, another meaning emerges. Some of us are white, and some of us are black. Until this year, the school has been almost exclusively white or near-white. I become identified with the white girls, because I am boarding. But I know my grandma looks like the grant-aid students, most of whom are day students and almost exclusively darker than the boarders. This is a big deal, though I don't understand why.

I notice almost all the teachers are white, many of them from England. I notice all the workers are black. I notice the school nurse is somewhere in the middle, closer to the workers than to the teachers, brown like Grandma. I take to faking stomachaches in the evenings so I can go see her after prep, the homework period, to get a spoonful of Barbie-pink, chalky-tasting Pepto-Bismol. I am usually one of the last to be picked up for half-term or other holidays, so I see the parents, or the drivers, who pick up my friends. Many of the parents are white; the drivers are black. Grandma and her cousins come and spill out of whoever's car has been borrowed for the trip. We are the colors of wet sand, coconut bark, soursop seed, and ground nutmeg. It is something of a miracle that my belongings and I can squeeze into the car. I am wedged against the window, between the sharp edges of the door and the cushioned contours of one of the many women I call "Aunt," though none of them really are. Half the time I don't understand what they are saying in rapid Jamaican patois; when I ask them to repeat things, they remind me that "children are to be seen, not heard." No one asks about school; the year I come in first in the class, they are late for the prize-giving, so no one sees. When I tell them about it, they remind me to work harder next year. I start to disappear through the car window, attach myself to the names of towns we pass through: Walker's Wood, Shooter's Hill, Brown's Town.

One holiday, I go to my friend Susan's house. Susan is white, the way that O. J. Simpson's daughter with Nicole is white: heavy golden hair, golden skin, light eyes. Their driver is black, and she calls him by his first name, although I have been taught to call men of his age "Mister." We pick up her brother at his boarding school; he is paler than she is, but has curly brown hair with his light eyes. We drive to the family house outside of Montego Bay, entering their private hillside through huge wrought-iron gates that declare the name in tall letters at the top: "Tara." The drive winds up through an avenue lined with palm trees that arch above us all the way to the clearing at the top of the hill, where a great white house dominates. I am awestruck by their home; the entry is larger than my grandma's entire house. Susan embraces a dark, round woman, not quite as old as my grandmother, and calls her "Judith." I know immediately that I cannot call her by her first name. All weekend, I wait for Susan to get thirsty or hungry, and add my request to hers in order to avoid asking Judith for anything directly. I revel in the house, especially the swimming pool, but dinner with the family is miserable: The mother is glamorous and whiny, the father preoccupied; the older brother boasts about social conquests; the younger one ignores everyone; and Susan and I moon about the house, listening to music, swimming, and one night, playing hide-and-seek on the grounds with flashlights and neighborhood children . . . all whitish, all protected, all free.

We are free, except for the one rule of the house: When we are outside, the Rhodesian ridgebacks must be in; when we are in, the dogs go out. One evening, as we're sitting in the library, one of the dogs gets in and makes a beeline for me. I'm small, he's big, but everyone is telling me not to be afraid. He doesn't like me, though, and I hear him growl. I take off like a rocket for the one room with a door I know I can find: Susan's. His claws clatter up the marble staircase right behind me until I slam the door in his face. I never ask outright whom the bad dogs are for.

Inhale—this is my body. Exhale—this is my home.

I spend two years at boarding school, and develop x-ray vision: I learn to see through surfaces. In D.C., we shop for my return trips at G.C. Murphy's, an ancestor of Wal-Mart, on Wisconsin Avenue. Pajamas, socks, bedding, goods for the elders: VO5, starlight mints, Preparation H, even a pressure cooker. I fly down alone, and tell the customs officer in Montego Bay that everything is for me. My mother's mixed feelings travel with me: When she was a young mother in Montego Bay, Susan's mother would cut her in public places. My mother says how nice it is I am making friends with the daughter, but I hear the poison of the remembered insult. At Grandma's, in St. Ann, I empty the suitcase of its cheap goods. We have a bad dog, too, but we keep him on a chain. We have an iron fence, too, but it's just the place where people stand, even when it is open, to call out to Grandma before entering. We have chickens and, once, a goat. Grandma cooks on an old kerosene stove so unreliable she makes me leave the kitchen when she lights it, in case it blows up. She tells stories about the families she worked for as a domestic in New York, in a tone that mixes disgust and admiration. She repeats one employer's observation—"Sylvia, she would say, I don't know why you would leave Jamaica and come here where everyone lives in fear!"—as if it represents all of them, and savors the implied envy.

One evening, I am in the front yard at Grandma's, hitting stones with a stick, when a voice comes across the fence: "What are you doing?"

"Playing baseball," I answer, faking an American identity I don't have. Barbara laughs and comes over, bringing her sister Meg. Kaye and Arlene come from across the street. We play freeze tag, and hide-and-seek, and jump rope. We are friends, but my best friend is the mango tree at the side of the house, behind the guava tree. Its branches are perfectly spaced to make a ladder for a nine-year-old, leading to two branches that serve as seat and backrest. I climb up with books borrowed from the library or Barbara's mother, and sit in the arms of this tree that demands nothing, judges nothing, is impossible to embarrass, filters the strong afternoon sun, and shares any passing breeze. I devour the imaginary worlds of Edith Nesbit's brave and lonely Railway Children, the lost children of Empire who find Frances Hodgson Burnett's Secret Garden and turn out to be Little Princesses. I admire Walter

Scott's second-place heroines, wild Flora and Rebecca, the Jewess, and I marvel at the adult-free worlds of Enid Blyton's characters, including the girls with boys' names: Roberta, known as Bobbie; Georgina, called George. I never question why our village looks different from theirs.

In treeworld, I am invisible, able to gaze as far as the gate, or India, or Scotland. Grandma grumbles about the mango stains on my clothes, but she likes that I am out of the way. One morning, I wake up and hear men's voices in the side yard. I rush outside to find a heavy gray sky, and all that is left of the tree is a stump. Grandma explains that it had to come down to make space to build a flat for my uncle. I am inconsolable; my world is always turning upside down and I never get to say goodbye.

When school reopens, we all pile into the car with my now-lightened suitcases, and drive up through the green mountains to the school and the dormitory. There I reunite with my friends who have never been to Grandma's, and we unpack together. I feel the glamour of the American goods emerging from my suitcase. I dimly realize that mention of Murphy's or lying to customs officers would tarnish the glamour, so I keep my mouth shut. We get down to the serious business of being girls on our own, making our own society of ins and outs, haves and have-nots, learning power and allegiance and betrayal. The headmistress is white and Victorian, but there are now brown teachers, and the head girl is darker and more dangerous than my grandma. I write a story for my final English exam, paying tribute to Blyton by naming streets after her and her characters. I pass at the top of my class, but not before a warning about suspicions that I have stolen my story. I am horrified to be so misunderstood, and I explain the limits of my borrowing. I insist that the story is mine, the streets mere decorations. But I no longer remember the story, only the warning.

When I come back to the United States to stay, we have moved into a one-bedroom garden apartment with a fancy zip code in Bethesda, Maryland. For the schools, my mother says. I am eleven and hate this new place. I am one of the poor kids attending the fancy public junior high school, and our bus numbers tell everyone where we are from. The first day, I miss the bus and arrive late, wearing shapeless clothes from Murphy's or the Junior League shop or one of those paper bags that appears in the night, dropped off by a friend who works as a domestic for a family with "girls my age." Other kids are wearing hip-hugger jeans, hot pants, and lip-gloss. I am so out of place, I never recover. I don't understand anything: a different teacher for every class, three-ring binders, bells and hall passes and cafeteria hierarchies.

I develop hives on my fingers, and can't imagine anyone ever wanting to hold my hand. My mother's beatings, which used to be limited by distance, become more frequent. I wear long sleeves on hot days to hide the welts. I am not sure what is being beaten into, or out of, my body. One message is that I am not free, like white people or people who are better off than we are. They can afford mistakes or stupidity or risks; we can't. Another is that I must not betray my mother or my family by behaving in some low-class way. Apparently, I'm getting both the white and the black beaten out of me, and what takes their place is a numbing certainty that there is no place for me in this world. I dream of death, preferably martyrdom. I will be diagnosed with incurable leukemia, and my final act will be to stand before the United Nations, as a child, and urge them toward world peace. They will weep with pity and recognition, and end all suffering. I develop a fascination with the Holocaust and the bombing of Hiroshima—what becomes of the survivors? I read John Hersey, Bruno Bettelheim, and Robert Jay Lifton as if my life depends on it, and perhaps it does. I feel like a displaced person from a war no one will admit to: between mother and daughter, rich and poor, immigrant and native, black and white. It is years before I will learn that my dilemmas were born on the plantation, and are not mine alone. Meanwhile, I fail my classes.

My mother then puts me in Catholic school, despite my resistance to attending a "snob school." The Ursuline nuns, as far as I can tell, are crazy. They encourage us to study independently, and no subject is off limits. I write papers on Lenin, on the Brontë sisters, on Graham Greene; I struggle in math. We learn there are three races: Caucasoid, Mongoloid, and

Negroid. My lousy math combines with misunderstood chemistry and racist anthropology: I imagine distilling my blood into seven parts white, one part black. Later, I figure out it is three to one, and I am what was called a quadroon. Others call me Spanish, Greek, Yugoslavian, Puerto Rican, their voices dropping as I dismiss them all; almost always, by the time people correctly guess, "Black?" they are whispering. I am both irritated and amused by their discomfort and bewilderment.

The school is half-black, half-white, with a handful of internationals. The school is also three-quarters rich, one-quarter poor, distributed across the races; all the internationals are well-off. Once more, I'm without an obvious place, but I make two friends, both working class, one black, one white, both American. Despite the nuns' best efforts—"Mingle, girls, mingle," they repeat in class after class—we tend to self-segregate. I wind up on everyone's margins, but I am not unhappy. It feels like a kind of freedom; although I do not know what to do with it, it has possibilities. I am becoming some kind of accordion: At school I expand, at home I contract.

My mother sends me to Grandma's in Jamaica for the summer because I am turning into too much of a "Yankee." Later, I realize it's simply more convenient to send me there than to figure out what to do with me in the States. I am a suitcase. All the relatives comment on how "clear" my complexion is. Self-absorbed as any adolescent, I think they are talking about blemishes, and I wonder why they are lying. I spend the summer reading Mills and Boone romances about independent women, seduced by the powerful men they work for, in exotic locations like Australia or Canada. It is my last summer "off."

The following summers, I baby-sit, run errands for a company selling answering machines, get a job in the medical records department of the Clinical Center, the hospital at the National Institutes of Health. I have the evening shift, where we pull the records for the following day's patients. We are the kind of motley crew I have come to take for granted in Washington: The supervisor is a white woman who has been there forever; her assistant, and the brains of the operation, is a black woman who has been there forever and a day. The rest of us are career government file clerks, graduate students, and high school students with college prospects. I identify with everyone, even the supervisor: She's a working woman. When the work slows, I read the patient histories in the charts. My desire for the stories of people's lives is insatiable, and I become very good at keeping secrets.

Then the white supervisor retires and they hire a young white woman with a library science degree from Indiana to replace her. I remember my shock, that they went all the way to Indiana to find someone, when they had a perfectly capable supervisor right here. They just didn't want to promote her because she was black. I tell my mother; we write the black representative from Maryland. There is a congressional investigation. The white girl still gets the job, but medical records and the laundry at NIH are condemned as segregated sweat-shops. My punishment is to be "disappeared." I spend my shifts alone in the medico-legal department, making copies for upcoming trials. The other workers are prohibited from talking to me. The director of the section finds me talking with a colleague at the water fountain one day and yells at me for what seems a long time. But I already know how to take a beating; I just wait for it to end.

This is the last relevant story of what I took for childhood: The Catholic archdiocese decides that it cannot support so many schools, and the one it decides to close is the one full of unpredictable nuns and girls. They sell Ursuline to the French International School, where I started so many years ago; I share the cafeteria with kids I knew in kindergarten, and we become friends again. Ursuline's eleventh and twelfth grades become a combined class. Since we will have enough credits to graduate by state standards, I am ready to finish high school at fifteen. Because of the combined class, the nuns decide to hold a competition for valedictorian. There are two competitors from the senior class: One is black, a winner of debate competitions throughout the region; the other is white. I am the sole representative of the junior class. I win the competition after delivering a speech based on that 1970s icon of heroic difference, Jonathan Livingston Seagull.

After graduation, I run into a white student from the senior class, who tells me the "real" story about my selection as valedictorian: When it seemed as if the black student might be the valedictorian for the last class graduating from Ursuline Academy, a number of white parents protested. I became the compromise candidate: I looked white on the outside, and only those who knew my story would know differently. My childhood ended that July afternoon, under the artificial daylight of the People's Drugstore at Wildwood Shopping Center on Old Georgetown Road where it meets Democracy Boulevard.

Inhale—this is my body. Exhale—this is my home.

Don't You Want to Sound Puerto Rican?

Esmeralda Santiago

One day, I returned from the library to find a woman and a girl about my age surrounded by my sisters and brothers, sipping coffee and chewing cake around the kitchen table.

"Guess who this is." Mami grinned.

The girl eyed me from under mascaraed lashes; the woman, petite, corseted, and skillfully made up, sized me up and found me deficient. I had no idea who they were and didn't care. "Friends from the factory?" I suggested, and Mami laughed.

"This is your sister Margie."

My mouth dropped in surprise, and I quickly closed it, because they laughed. Margie, her mother, Provi, my sisters and brothers, who were bunched on the side of the table closest to Margie, all seemed to think it was hilarious that I didn't recognize someone I didn't remember meeting.

"She's got the most expressive face," Provi giggled, and my cheeks burned. Mami crinkled her eyes at me and tipped her head toward Margie and Provi. I touched each one's shoulders with my fingertips, leaving lots of space between us, and kissed them lightly on the right cheek.

Provi had been my father's "wife" before he met my mother. I'd expected Margie to look like our father, with his high forehead, prominent cheekbones, broad nose, full lips. I'd expected his coloring, but she was lighter and looked more like my sister Norma, with the same tightly curled auburn hair, slanted brown eyes, regal bearing.

Mami served me coffee and cake. "Provi brought it from a bakery near her apartment in Manhattan." It sounded like a warning, but when I looked up, Mami's back was to me as she refilled her coffee cup.

Margie was uncomfortable at our table, her back to the wall, as my sisters and brothers jostled and pushed one another to stand the closest to her. Héctor brought out his entire bottle cap collection, and Edna drew flowers and birds and offered them for Margie's approval. Every once in a while, Margie smiled at me, and I wished we could go somewhere and talk. But there was no other place, no living room, no yard, no room that wasn't filled with beds or people. I was embarrassed and tried to read Mami's feelings. But she was serene, didn't seem to notice that Provi's eyes darted from the sink stacked with clean but battered pots and pans to the next room, where a rope was strung from the window to the door-jamb. Under it, water dripped onto the dull linoleum from the diapers up to dry. Every once in a while, Delsa grabbed the mop, soaked up the puddles, then pushed her way back to Margie's side.

I was annoyed at Mami's composure. She should have been as ashamed as I felt. As soon as the thought surfaced, I banished it. Mami worked hard for us, and while I had less than I wanted, as the eldest I got more than my younger sisters and brothers. When they complained that Mami favored me, I argued that she didn't; but inside I knew she did, as did Tata. I settled back on my chair, seething, alternating shame with guilt, envious of Margie's fashionable clothes; her rolled, teased, sprayed hair; her meticulous makeup; the charm bracelet that tinkled on her right wrist, the Timex on her left. At the same time, I longed to talk to her, to find out if she was in touch with Papi, if it hurt when he remarried, if she remembered our grandmother, whom, Provi said, I resembled.

Mami spoke with pride about how much English we'd learned in a scant two years, about the school I attended, about how sweet-natured baby Franky was, about her job as a Merrow sewing machine operator in a Maidenform factory. The two of them talked as if they were long-lost friends, when in fact for years Mami referred to Provi as "that woman," and Provi must have had a few names for Mami when she wasn't sitting at our kitchen table drinking coffee and delicately chewing the too-sweet cake she'd brought.

Provi boasted about their apartment in Manhattan, where, she pointed out, Margie had her own room. About how Margie was one of the top students in her school, about how they'd lived in the United States so long, they were for-getting their Spanish while still learning English.

"And then what do we do?" she cackled. "We'll be mute, with nothing to say!" Mami and I exchanged a look, remem-bering our far-from-speechless La Muda.

I interpreted Provi's friendliness as an act. Used to the drama student's obsession with finding subtext in dialogue, I listened to Provi chatter but heard the unspoken "You weren't woman enough to hold on to Pablo," while Mami's unsaid "I had him for fourteen years, four times longer than you did" heated the air.

I imagined Provi was glad Mami was widowed, saw her son Francisco's death as punishment for the wrong I guessed Mami had done her. Mami, younger and prettier, was, I sus-pected, the reason Papi had left Provi.

I sulked at my end of the table, listened to our mothers babble, aware they were still competing for my father, who wasn't there, who was married to another woman neither one of them had met. I heard nothing but criticism in Provi's remarks, only defenses in Mami's. I pitied Margie, whose shoulders slumped into the chair, as if she too was embar-rassed by her mother's behavior. I resisted Provi's tight smiles and Margie's frequent attempts to make eye contact. Every second of their visit was a test we had to pass to rise to another level, but I wasn't sure what that level was, where it lay, if it existed. Margie had come too late, but I didn't know what she was late for, or whether and why I'd been waiting for her.

As Mami closed the door after them, she breathed a deep sigh. My sisters and brothers scattered to other parts of the apartment. Tata, who stayed in her room during the entire visit, stumbled into the kitchen and began chopping onions for the night's supper.

"Isn't Margie pretty?" Mami asked, not expecting an answer. Tata grumbled about "that woman." I was about to make a sarcastic remark but decided against it.

"She has nice hair," I allowed. "I like the way she lines her eyes with the little tail at the corner," I added, to say something nice, and Mami fixed her gaze on me, as if seeing what wasn't obvious before.

"You have better hair," she said, running her fingers through it. "It's wavy, not so curly as hers. You can do more with it." She took my face in her hands, tipped it to the light. "As for her makeup, that line wouldn't look good on you. Your eyes are a completely different shape." She pushed my face to the left, to the right. "Maybe if the tail were shorter . . . Why don't you try it?"

I dashed to the dresser where she kept the cosmetics she hadn't worn since Francisco's death. Breathless, I opened the zippered pouch. Inside, there was a mirrored plastic compact with a thin circle of pressed powder around the metal bottom, the once fluffy cotton pad flat and frayed around the edges.

A smaller, round cardboard box held her powdered rouge, which leaked a fine red dust over two lipsticks and a stubby eyebrow pencil. I uncapped the point, whittled the wood with a Gem blade, and drew a curve on the back of my hand. When I tried it on my lid, the hard point slipped and left a faint ashen stripe, which I wiped with spit and toilet tissue. When I finally got it to sketch a dark line on my upper lid, I extended it to a jaunty angle, like a smile.

"What do you think?" I tried to still the thumps inside my chest that betrayed my excitement. Mami leaned against the counter, squinting as if evaluating an expensive purchase.

"It looks nice," she said. "But next time, make the tails shorter."

"Okay." Next time, she said. Next time! I ran back to the bathroom, erased the ends of the lines so that they didn't extend beyond the lids.

"Like this?"

"Perfect," she smiled. "That looks nice."

Tata watched from her post by the stove. "She's growing up," she said softly, and I pleaded for silence with my eyes. She turned with a grin. Mami smiled and went back to washing the rice.

In my room I stared at the reflection, fingered the thick dark lines around my eyes that made me look older, sophisticated. Delsa was in my bed, wrapped in a blanket, her black curls peeking through the top.

"Quit it," she mumbled, though I hadn't made a sound. I left the room, curled up against the wall on Norma and Alicia's bed, and watched television. My eyes felt heavy, as if the black line added weight to them. During a commercial, Alicia stared hard at me, then trotted to the kitchen yelling, "Mami, Negi is wearing makeup."

"Shut up," I rushed after her and held her back.

"What's all the shouting?" Mami called.

"Negi's wearing makeup," Alicia repeated, fighting me.

"Leave your sister alone," Mami yelled, and I wasn't sure if she meant me or Alicia. "Next time I go to a drugstore," she said over her shoulder as she headed back, "I'll buy you your own pencil."

I let go of Alicia, who looked from me to Mami with a puzzled expression. She was nine, I was fifteen, and although Mami took my side in many arguments with my sisters and brothers, we both knew that something important had happened. I stopped being a little girl because Mami wouldn't be outmothered by Provi.

It was always still dark when I left the apartment at five-thirty in the morning, my books and dance clothes in La Muda's old black leather bag. The fifteen-minute walk to the elevated train station was a gauntlet of shadows under burnt-out street lamps that lengthened the distance between abandoned buildings and parked cars. I walked in the middle of the sidewalk, eyes fixed straight ahead but alert, expecting danger from any direction at any moment. Once, a rat scurried in front of me. I didn't know what to do, afraid to walk, afraid to stand in the same spot. After a few seconds, I ran past the pile of garbage into which the rat had disappeared and added "bit by a rabid rat" to the list of *algos* that could happen away from home.

Even at six in the morning the trains were packed, and I often stood most of the way into Manhattan. This morning, I was lucky. When the train came, I spotted a space in the two-seater bench across from the conductor's booth. I took it, careful not to disturb the woman who slept on the seat closest to the door, her gloved hands pressed against a handbag on her lap. The passengers already on the train were black and Puerto Rican, but as we moved from East New York to Brownsville into Crown Heights, Prospect Heights, and Brooklyn Heights, the people waiting at the platforms were white and older than the passengers on board. They pushed into the subway car as everyone squeezed together to make room.

A man elbowed his way toward the hang-strap above where I sat against the wall. He set his briefcase on the floor between his legs, grabbed the hang-strap with his left hand, unbuttoned and pulled open his coat, his right hand in the pocket. I kept my eyes on my book, only dimly aware of the movement in front of me, until I realized that he was leaning in so close that he blocked the light. When I looked up to ask him to move, I saw that his zipper was open and his penis dangled outside his pants, not two feet from my face. I quickly looked down at my book, too embarrassed to say or do anything. His coat formed a curtain on one side, and the wall trapped me on the other. I pretended to read while I tried to figure out what to do. I could get up and move, but my bag was under my feet, and if I bent down to reach it, I'd be dangerously close to his wan, wrinkled penis. I considered but didn't have the nerve to look him in the eye and tell him to put it back where it belonged. As we reached a station and the train slowed, he dropped his arm from the hang-strap, covered himself, and waited until the train was moving, then raised his arm so his penis was again in my face. I felt him stare while I struggled with what to do. I could grab the penis and pull hard. I could bite it. Without touching it, I could slam the pages of my biology text around it. But I sat stony-faced and silent, pretending to read, angry that I was being such a *pendeja*, wondering what I'd done to provoke him.

Theatrical makeup was taught in a room across from the auditorium's backstage entrance. The teacher, Mrs. Bank, a no-nonsense woman with a reputation for being exacting and difficult to please, was nevertheless beloved by those students who managed to impress her with their talent. I wasn't among her favorites. I had too little range as an actress to meet her high standards.

During her first class, she gave us a list of supplies, and I had to convince Mami the expense was necessary, that make-up was a real course in which I'd be graded. She frowned at the brushes and pencils, sponges, puffs, powders, and creams that cost more than what she put on her face. But she never said I couldn't have it.

Mrs. Bank moved us quickly through the rudiments of stage makeup. We began with techniques to enhance our natural features. Boys as well as girls were taught to apply foundation, lip liner, cheek color, and mascara. We were encouraged to study our faces, to learn their contours, to examine the shapes that made up our appearance, to look at ourselves not as who we were, but as who we could become.

To this end, we were taught to alter our features. Through skillful use of highlights and shadows, we learned to narrow a broad nose and to flatten a pointy one. Eyes could be made larger, lips fuller, flat cheekbones rounded, high foreheads lowered.

I loved the class because I could apply as much makeup as I wanted and Mami couldn't complain, since I told her it was my homework to practice. I spent hours in front of the mirror making myself up to look innocent, sultry, elegant, Chinese. One of the assignments was to bring in a picture of an animal and to recreate the animal's features on my own face. At home, I made myself up as a tiger, a camel, an orangutan, then chased my sisters and brothers around the apartment, making the appropriate animal sounds until Mami or Tata put an end to my grunts and their screams.

One of the last assignments of the semester was to make ourselves up as old people.

"Follow the natural contours of your face," Mrs. Bank instructed. "Darken the creases from your nostrils to your lips. Highlight along the edges to deepen them."

Most of us were fifteen or sixteen years old, and finding wrinkles in our faces was difficult, not because they weren't there, but because we didn't want them to be.

"If you pucker your lips like this, then draw lines where the puckers are, you'll get some interesting wrinkles."

We followed her instructions, giggling as our faces aged under puffs and brushes.

"Most people have lines around their eyes," she pointed out. "Don't forget your neck and hands; they age, too."

We drew liver spots on the backs of our hands. We powdered our hair to make it white. Jay applied a wart to his cheek. Elaine practiced a quiver in her voice to go with her frail, old-lady face.

At the end of class, when Mrs. Bank asked us to evaluate the work we'd done, I looked closely at my wrinkled cheeks, at the curious eyes inside deep circles, and burst into tears.

"What's the matter?" Mrs. Bank asked, alarmed.

"I'm an old lady," I whined in what I thought was a playful manner, to cover up my embarrassment.

Mrs. Bank smiled. "Not quite, not yet. Lucky for you, it disappears with Albolene cream."

"That's good," I giggled listlessly. "I'm too young to be old."

She moved on. I faced the mirror again and saw my grandmother, Abuela, whom I hadn't seen in three years. But if I turned to the left, there was Tata, the grandmother I lived with. It was frightening to see them both staring at me from my own face. Abuela's sad eyes, Tata's sensual mouth, Abuela's small nose, Tata's intelligent gaze. But I wouldn't admit that to Mrs. Bank or the other students who laughed at my fear of growing old. Let them think what they will. They will never know— they can't even understand—who I really am.

I had a secret life, one not shared with my sister, with whom I shared a bed. Or with my classmates, with whom I shared dreams of fame and fortune. Not with my mother, whose dreams were on hold since Francisco's death. My secret life was in my head, lived at night before I fell asleep, when I became someone else.

In my secret life I wasn't Esmeralda Santiago, not Negi, not a scared Puerto Rican girl, but a confident, powerful woman whose name I changed as I tried to form the perfect me. Esme, I was once. Emmé, another time. Emeraude, my French class name. I tried Shirley, Sheila, Lenore, but names not based on my own didn't sound quite right. So I was Emma, Ralda, or just plain E.

In these dreams, I had no family—no mother or father, no sisters or brothers, no grandmothers, no wrestling cousins, no drunk uncles. I was alone, sprung from an unnameable darkness, with no attachments, no loyalties, no responsibilities. I was educated, successful, professional. Whatever I did, I did well, with no false steps, no errors, no embarrassing mistakes that caused others to judge or to laugh at me.

I was the pilot of my own plane and flew around the world, and everywhere I went people were happy to see me and no one asked where I was from. I was a movie star, and my character never died. I was a scientist, surrounded by test tubes and beakers, Bunsen burners hissing blue flames as I received the Nobel Prize.

In my secret life, I drove a convertible, and my house at the end of a long, sinuous highway overlooked miles of green, rolling hills where it never snowed. I lived alone in my hilltop house, surrounded by books that I didn't have to return to the library. And every room was tidy, though I never cleaned.

In my secret life, I wasn't Puerto Rican. I wasn't American. I wasn't anything. I spoke every language in the world, so I was never confused about what people said and could be understood by everyone. My skin was no particular color, so I didn't stand out as black, white, or brown.

I lived this secret life every night as I dozed into sleep, and every morning I resisted opening my eyes to the narrow bed in the narrow room that I shared with Delsa, my chest tight with surprise and disappointment that it was all a dream.

"Eee, eee, eee, eee." I enunciated the vowels as Dr. Dycke, the head of the drama department, instructed. "Ay, ay, ay, ay. Eee, eee, eee, eee."

Raymond peeked around the doorjamb. "What you doin'?"

"Practicing. Eee, ay, eee, ay, eee."

"Why?"

"So I can learn to speak English without an accent."

"Oh." He went away.

"Eee, eee, ay, ay, eee, eee, ay, ay."

A few minutes later Edna appeared at the door. "What you doin'?"

"Practicing. Eee, eee, eee."

"Practicing what?"

"Ask Raymond!" I closed the door on her face. "Ay. Ay. Ay. Oo. Oo. Oo." The door opened. "Gettatta here!" I screamed, then, "Oh, it's you."

"I have to find something." Delsa pointed at the dresser.

I backed up and let her through. "Eeu. Oo. Eeu. Oo. Ay."

"What *are* you doing?" She pulled a clean shirt from the drawer.

"That's it." I pushed her into the front room. "Everybody here!" I shouted. "Héctor! Norma! Mami! Tata!"

"What do you want?" Norma called from the back of the apartment.

Mami appeared from the kitchen. "What's all the yelling?"

"I want everyone here, so I can say this once."

"Say what?" Raymond asked.

"Norma! Héctor! Alicia! Get over here!"

"Quiet," Mami snapped. "Franky's sleeping."

"Hold on. I'm not as fast as I used to be." Tata shuffled toward the front room.

As everyone settled on the beds, the floor, the sofa, I began. "I have a class called voice and diction where I'm learning to talk without an accent."

"Why? Don't you want to sound Puerto Rican?" Héctor smirked.

"Let her speak," Tata said.

"It's part of my schoolwork," I pierced Héctor with a look.

"It sounded like you were imitating animals," Edna scoffed, and everyone laughed.

"Ha, ha, very funny." Unsmiling, I waited for them to settle. "I have to practice, and I can't have you interrupt me every five seconds to ask what I'm doing. So if you hear any weird sounds coming from the room, I'm doing my homework. Okay?"

"Is this what the yelling was about?" Mami asked.

"Yes. The kids were bothering me." I glared at Edna, Raymond, and Delsa. They looked at Mami, who stared at me hard. For a minute, she seemed about to scold me for making a big fuss out of nothing. But she turned to the kids.

"Let your sister be when she's doing her homework," she warned.

"It sounds like a zoo in here," Norma protested.

"Go to the other side of the apartment when she's practicing."

I backed into the bedroom, followed by Norma's, "But it's not fair."

It wasn't. Since I started Performing Arts High School, Mami favored me. If I was reading and complained that the television was too loud, she made the kids turn it down. If I wanted to go to bed early, everyone was moved to the kitchen, where they could make a racket and I wouldn't hear. If I brought home a list of school supplies, Mami didn't say we had no money. She gave me enough to buy them, or she'd get them for me without complaining about the cost. I knew how hard she worked to support us, so I didn't abuse her. But I felt guilty that so much of what little we had was spent on me. And I dreaded the price.

"I live for my children," Mami asserted. I was certain that no matter how hard I worked, I'd never be able to repay all she'd given up so that I could have what I needed.

Mami had dropped out of elementary school and didn't let us forget what a mistake she had made by not pursuing an education. While she never complained that we were a burden, her voice quivered when she told us it would be hard to be both mother and father to eight children. Although she never talked about them, she must have had dreams once. But I was born, and every year after that when one of my brothers or sisters was born, those dreams ebbed further and further as she focused on making sure we had dreams of our own.

"What do you want to be when you grow up?" she'd ask.

"A doctor," Delsa answered. She had high marks in school, better than mine, especially in math and science. And it was more likely that she'd be a doctor than that I'd ever be a good actress.

"A racecar driver," Héctor announced, his eyes bright, his hands around an invisible steering wheel. At eleven years old, Héctor already worked at the pizzeria next door. Every few days, he brought home a couple of pizzas with plenty of sausages and pepperoni that Gino, the owner, gave him.

"Your son is a good worker," Gino told Mami. "You raised him right." Mami beamed at the compliment, and Héctor worked harder. At the end of the week, he gave Mami most of what he'd earned.

"And you, Raymond," Mami urged, "what do you want to be when you grow up?"

"A policeman," Raymond responded. "And I'll give you a ticket if you drive fast on my street," he warned Héctor. Raymond's foot, after three years of treatments, had healed, his limp gone. It was easy to imagine him in uniform, strutting down the street, looking for bad guys.

"I'll have my own beauty parlor," Alicia declared. At nine, Alicia already knew how to form her thick, black, wavy hair into many styles by the skillful use of a brush, comb, and bobby pins. "And I'll give you a permanent for free!"

Edna, who spent hours drawing curvaceous women in bizarre outfits, added, "I'm going to have a dress store. And you can get all the clothes you want. For free!"

"Wow! I'm going to be a rich old woman," Mami laughed, and we giggled at the image of Mami being old. It was impossible to imagine she'd ever look any different than she looked then, her black hair tousled, her curls hugging her freckled cheeks.

When we talked like this, Don Julio and Tata watched with bemused expressions, as if they could see into the future and knew what our lives would really be like. They, unlike Mami, were old, and even through the haze of cigarette smoke that surrounded them and the slurred speech after too much beer or wine, they seemed wise in a way Mami didn't.

"Don't count your chickens . . ." Tata began, and she didn't have to finish to confirm what I'd already learned was true: that to announce what was to be was to jinx it.

Mami, Tata, and Don Julio often told me how smart I was, but I interpreted their comments without thinking. My grades were average to low, and I'd failed geometry, which meant summer school and no job. I'd learned English quickly, but that was no surprise, since at Performing Arts we analyzed, memorized, and recited some of the best works written in the English language. My sisters and brothers hadn't the benefit of Performing Arts and could speak the language as well as I did, though with a Brooklyn accent.

Mami was proud I went into the city every day by myself, returned when expected, was watchful that *algo* wouldn't happen. But I never admitted how scared I was early in the morning walking down our dark streets to the subway. I didn't mention that men exposed themselves, that sometimes they took advantage of a crowded subway to press themselves against me, or to let their hands wander to parts of my body no one should touch unless I asked them to. I didn't report the time I was chased from the subway station to the door of the school by a woman waving an umbrella and screaming, "Dirty spick, dirty fucking spick, get off my street." I never told Mami that I was ashamed of where we lived, that in the *Daily News* and the *Herald*

211

American, government officials called our neighborhood "the ghetto," our apartment building "a tenement." I swallowed the humiliation when those same newspapers, if they carried a story with the term "Puerto Rican" in it, were usually describing a criminal. I didn't tell Mami that although she had high expectations for us, outside our door, the expectations were lower, that the rest of New York viewed us as dirty spicks, potential muggers, drug dealers, prostitutes.

Mami was happy that I, at sixteen years of age, and now *casi mujer,* almost a woman, showed no interest in boys.

"She's too smart to get involved with those good-for-nothings around here," she asserted, when she knew I was listening.

And I didn't argue, although quality was not the issue. There were no boys my age in our neighborhood. And in school, some of the boys were homosexual, while those who weren't had no interest in girls like me. I was poor, talented enough not to embarrass myself on a stage, but only good enough to play Cleopatra and other exotic characters. When the subject of dating came up in social studies class, I admitted that my mother didn't allow me to date unless chaperoned. That insured no boy in the entire grade would ask. What was the point? If I asked Mami to let me date, I'd get a lecture about how boys only want one thing, and I wasn't willing to give it to anyone. All I had to do was look around me to know what happened to a girl who let a man take the place of an education.

In the cramped, noisy apartment where my mother struggled to keep us safe, where my grandmother tried to obliterate her pain with alcohol, where my sisters and brother planned and invented their futures, I improvised. When it hurt, I cried silent tears. And when good things came my way, I accepted them gratefully but quietly, afraid that enjoying them too much would make them vanish like a drop of water into a desert.

An Apology to Althea Connor:
Private Memory and the Ethics of Public Memoir

Traise Yamamoto

I.

It is 1972, just barely in the aftermath of the Civil Rights movement and in the midst of school desegregation. I am in fifth grade at a public elementary school in the Bay Area. The school pulls from several neighborhoods and combines a heavily Latino population from the East Side with the almost all-white population of the Piedmont Hills area. It is a new class for me, since I have just moved from another city. As usual, I am the only Asian American in my class of fifth-graders, which, for some reason, is nearly totally white. I notice an African American girl in a bright pink dress (her favorite, as I will find out later) at the back of the room. Her name is Althea Connor. Over the next few weeks, we will become friends, then best friends. And then . . .

But I jump ahead of my narrative. When I was growing up, I learned early, as do most children of color, that being who I was different from being white. Much of the time, as a young child, this was neither here nor there. I could not imagine a life in which there was no Bon Odori to look forward to every summer, with its clucking community of Buddhist church ladies shooing us away, a life in which dinner tables were absent of rice, takuan, tofu. But it also meant knowing—it seems knowing always—about the internment, about why both my grandfathers were gardeners, why my grandmother cleaned other people's houses. Somehow this all seemed part of familial knowledge.

But my entry into public school introduced me firsthand to what being Asian (the American part always forgotten or ignored) meant to other children: little blonde, blue-eyed girls saying I cannot sit next to them on the bus; schoolmates pulling the edges of their eyes, bucking their teeth, and shouting out the public language of racial othering: jap, chink, go back where you came from chinaman, slitty eyes, japjapjap.

By the time I walked into that classroom, where Althea sat in the back, my sense of being Japanese American was connected to the current U.S. war in Vietnam, which had become a strange but insistent part of my consciousness. We had recently moved from Cupertino, a largely white suburb that was primarily working class and where most people in our neighborhood were just trying to figure out how to make a decent living. But my grandmother had insistently warned my mother not to wear her pagoda-shaped straw hat while she worked in the yard, fearing that our neighbors might mistake her for Viet Cong and shoot her on the front lawn, right there in Cupertino, California—where our landlord had once accused us of bringing the cockroaches my mother insisted he do something to get rid of. I didn't know exactly what a cockroach was, but I imagined us at our old house carefully putting our personal horde of roaches into plastic bags, packing the bags into boxes, then setting them free into the great wild of the next rental house. It wasn't until my parents fought about my father not saying anything back to the landlord that I had understood just what he had suggested about us. "You," I remember my mother screaming at my father, "have no backbone, just because he's a *hakujin*. He basically says we live in filth, and you don't say anything!" What was hard to understand then, and even now, is how much of her criticism of him had to do with the private tensions between them (they would eventually divorce) and how much registered a broader landscape of racial tensions. Did my father truly have no backbone, or was my mother just haranguing him? If he deferred, was it a strategic response to hostile white people? Or was yelling at my father my mother's only way of registering her frustration at society's racism? Whatever it was, I understood there was some affect my mother desired my father to have, but which he apparently lacked.

Already, at age ten, Althea had presence, that kind of held-back dignity some young girls have and, if they're lucky, keep past puberty. And she watched. I watched her watching.

Pretty soon we started talking—Althea really wasn't the type to play. She told me there was a new, Black way of talking. "'Good' means bad, but 'bad' means good," she said. I didn't quite believe her, but I was willing to allow that the idea of switching words around was at least interesting. As the weeks went on, she told me about what Black people were doing to change the country and how I could be a part of it, too, since I wasn't white. For the first time in my life, someone connected the kinds of things that had happened to me on numerous schoolyard playgrounds with what had happened to others who were not white. For the first time, I was listening to someone who put race at the center of her thinking. It was from Althea that I learned about systemic racism, though she didn't use that term. She talked about Black Power and about white folks keeping Black people down, or trying to, and she connected that to my experiences of name-calling and exclusion. Thus, one of the most important things I learned that year in fifth grade was a language for talking about racism in more than personal and private terms. I learned about systemic oppression, and I learned that talking about it was a way of fighting it.

At recess, we would chatter on about how we wanted to decorate our rooms, what colors we liked best (Althea was big on appropriate decorative accoutrements). And with that talent children have for the abrupt conversational shift, we'd segue straight from the virtues of strawberry-scented candles to how Black people were going to revolutionize the United States with other non-honkies—another new word whose meaning I wondered at, being the literal girl I was. (White people beeped their car horns at non-white people? Was it based on some special code word *hakujins* used with each other?) I was as taken with the reinvention of language that Althea was telling me about as I was with the idea that there was a whole community out there that whites were not and could not be part of.

As the weeks progressed, our playground discussions with each other became increasingly public. Other children would see us in intense conversation and want to know what we were talking about, or they might start to eavesdrop if they were playing nearby. Of course, we soon noticed that we were getting our schoolmates' attention, and we duly accommodated them. Pretty soon we were sitting atop the climbing structure talking about the history of racism: Althea would begin with forced removal and slavery, I would pick up with the internment during World War II, and Althea would finish up with the Civil Rights movement. It was heady stuff: a handful of our white classmates listening to how They had wronged Us. When I think of those images now, they strike me as both comical and amazing: two skinny ten-year-olds agitating and testifying atop the monkey bars.

As might be expected, parents soon got wind of what their children were doing during recess, and they weren't happy about it. Eventually, some of those parents called the teacher, and the teacher called my mother. From what I was able to piece together at the time and in the years since, I was not considered by my teacher to be a co-conspirator. Rather, I was under a bad influence and was beginning to develop "a chip on my shoulder." It was causing me to not get along with my peers in a manner my teacher found concerning. Even now, my mother, no stranger to standing up and speaking out where racism is concerned, insists that there is a difference between being aware of racism and "going out of your way to look for it," and that the latter identified what Althea was doing. I have often wondered whether my mother has ever considered that her response to my teacher might have borne some resemblance to the interaction between my father and that landlord.

The upshot was that I was forbidden to be friends with Althea. At home, I was no longer allowed to talk to her on the phone. At school, my desk was moved across the room from hers, and we were not to play with each other at recess. In short order, our classmates, never that taken with Althea in the first place, didn't just ignore her, but began actively to exclude her in those subtle but unmistakably cruel ways children do. She was completely isolated: No one talked to her unless they were harassing her; no one ate lunch with her or played with her at recess. I would steal glances over at Althea from my seat in class. She either stared stonily ahead or absorbed herself with some task at hand. This stoicism seemed to inspire not less but more taunting and exclusionary behavior from the other children.

And what did I do in response? In the world of sitcoms and the Disney Channel, I would have silently but cogently watched what was happening, a sense of injustice stirring within. My sense of righteous anger would build steadily until, spurred by that one proverbial excess straw, I would fling parental and teacherly directives aside and come to the defense of my friend. The fact is, I did nothing. If I did not go so far as to join in with the vengeful teasing meant to put Althea back in her place, I did the next worst thing, which was to do nothing to stop it. There was a definitive difference in how each of us was dealt with, and this difference had everything to do with race: Althea was the perpetrator who needed disciplinary action. I was the usually compliant Japanese American girl whose quest for good grades was unfortunately interrupted by a radically inappropriate influence. I merely needed to be redirected; Althea needed to be broken. I don't recall our teacher doing anything to intervene between Althea and the rest of the class.

After a few weeks, Althea Connor was suddenly no longer there. At first I thought she had been moved to another class, but I never saw her again. I saw her mother once after that. She must have been at school to pick up Althea's things or to sign paperwork of some kind. She saw me, and even now I remember the directness and complexity of the look on her face: There was anger, but also grief, disappointment, and the acknowledgment that it both was and wasn't my fault. Somehow, I learned that she and Mr. Connor had put Althea in a private school.

Althea was a crucial figure in my coming to an analysis and understanding of racism. I have often returned to these memories with a mix of guilt and gratitude, thankful that Althea taught me what she knew, regretting that there is no way for me to tell her that. But there has always been an unidentified unease. It has not been until recently that I understood why.

If I turn the angle of memory and think not about how I benefited from my conversations with Althea, but rather why she inaugurated them, those talks take on a very different meaning. Even at that early age, she knew she needed allies—not just in the obvious sense, but in a deeper way, in the sense of having someone else who understood her language. Just as she needed someone else to know that "good" meant bad and "bad" meant good, she needed someone else who spoke her language about racism and social oppression. She needed to carve out a space for herself in what was otherwise an indifferent to hostile environment. She was the only African American in our class, and as I recall, there were not many African Americans in the entire school. If I think about those talks from a different angle, what strikes me is not what I learned from them or how I gained an analytical framework from them, but rather what they cost Althea—both in terms of what eventually happened and in terms of what had necessitated her knowledge in the first place. From my perspective now as an adult, I admire Althea for doing what she had to do to make a space for herself, but it also pains me that already, at age ten, she knew what strategies she would need for her own psychic survival. And from my perspective now as a mother, I see what it meant that her parents had already had to give her the tools to understand her situation, as well as the tools to protect herself from it.

So this working-through, this foregrounding I offer as both analysis and apology, even as something in me refuses the expiation of guilt through public spectacle. Even here, I risk turning Althea into a Black icon of my own evolving consciousness. But what happened to her was wrong and it was cruel, not least because, amongst all else, she was only a child. The disjunctions between the private and the public have never felt greater than now, because it is to that child that I want to apologize—for my cowardice and my complicity—but I also know that to reprivatize what happened through only personal apology would be to reenact my own angles and omissions of memory. So it is at the seam of, or rather the overlap between, the private and the public that I address this utterance, this acknowledgment, this apology, this attempt to speak a public language.

II.

A few weeks after the academic conference for which the preceding section was originally written (and which has been modified here), I found Althea. I had tried to locate her beforehand, interested in what her version of events would be, and curious, as I had been for almost thirty years, to find out what had become of her. I finally found her in the most banal of ways: through a Web search. It turns out that the two ten-year-old girls who lectured their classmates on the playground have both gone on to become professors, habitués of academia, a jungle gym of its own sort. But there our similarities end.

At this point, I would ask you to assess your response to my narrative, to my self-representation, and, most importantly, to my representation of Althea Connor. From the responses I have received so far, my guess is that, in the lingo of the fifth grade, you are on her side, indignant over what happened. That is, she is a sympathetic subject. If this is the case, ask yourself why.

Because the next thing I'll tell you about Althea is that she grew up to become a conservative apologist for Reagan-era international politics, one who received her doctorate from an Ivy League institution and has had an extremely successful career, including stints at the prestigious conservative think tank, the Hoover Institution, where she has associated with the likes of Shelby Steele and Condoleezza Rice. She has been appointed to the U.S. Defense Policy Board. "Althea Connor" is also a pseudonym.

After establishing email contact, at which Althea declared herself delighted because she had often thought of me, I told her why I had been thinking of her with particular intensity of late, and I sent her the paper. Her reaction, as might be indicated by her specialty in international relations and national security, was swift, decisive, and unambiguous. She was, insofar as the cold type of email can register tonal nuance, furious. She disagreed completely with my narrative of what had happened, in terms of both details and intensity. She questioned my memory, my motives, and my methodology—of which she opined there was none—and felt that all I had done was to provide yet another example of a victimized Black person. This story, she went on, was not only well rehearsed, but had been narrated much more brilliantly by others. She averred that I no doubt had a right to my own memories, but that she did not wish to be the vehicle through which I worked out my particular and personal "problems." Finally, she ended by demanding to know where and when I had given the paper and threatening to contact any journal in which I might publish it. She would, she said, tell them that she objected to her name being used and that what I wrote was a false representation and not in line with anything that she remembered.

I wrote back and assured Althea that I would be happy to use a pseudonym and I would neither quote directly from her emails nor include any specific information that might easily identify her. When I offered that she could choose a pseudonym, she answered that I must not have understood her desire to have nothing to do with my article, and that even agreeing to the use of a pseudonym would imply assent to my version of what had happened and that it represented her in some way. After a very long email in which I apologized for upsetting her and explained my narrative, what I was trying to do, and so on, our exchange ceased.

In the aftermath of my contact with Althea, what had originally been a paper focused on thinking through the identifications and differences between African Americans and Asian Americans has become an exploration into the politics of memory, the representation of the past, and the moral dimensions of autobiographical writing.

For one, how do we react to someone who turns out not to be a "good" subject? Althea's neoconservatism certainly doesn't make her easy for some of us to like. More disturbingly, however, it may tempt us into easy and seemingly logical claims that what happened all those years ago, at least as I described it, clearly contributed to Althea's present neocon, no-victims-here stance. But such suppositions seem to me disrespectful and profoundly presumptuous, not least because they stem from the assumption that reactionary politics and an overall conservatism, especially in a person of color, can only be explained in terms of pathology. Notwithstanding my own political leanings, and however much I might be tempted to indulge in the satisfying sentiment of sniffing dismissal, the danger of such causal explanations is that they always function within a political paradigm in which the rightness of the good/the liberal/the Left is self-evident and in which the bad/the reactionary/the Right is discussed in terms that foreclose the possibility of complexity or authentic self-awareness in those of the latter persuasion.

This last point touches on the ethical and moral dimensions of personal narratives and their use in theorizing, especially when doing so involves resistant subjects or those who do not readily conform to one's own notion of the "good subject." Autobiography has become a key narrative form for minoritized communities because there has been growing recognition of the ways in which the experiential and personal crucially inform our critical and theoretical positions. But autobiographical narratives written by "othered" writers have always had to balance very carefully between individuality and representativeness, to speak from a very specific personal experience while also representing—whether by choice or default—the communities with which the writer is identified. But how much more difficult and fraught is this process when the "us" for whom one speaks—through the public act of writing—is not at all commensurate with who "we" understand "ourselves" to be? Although many accept that one's sense of self is not constructed in a vacuum and that, therefore, to speak of the self and how it came to be is inevitably to speak of others, what are we to do when personal narratives include other people who may not want to be narrated, who may not wish to be spoken?

From Althea's point of view, however "good" I thought my motives, the fact is that I have either dredged up events that so clash with her present sense of self as to be extremely painful, or I have constructed an event and a persona that have little to do with who she considers herself to be but with which she must nevertheless deal, and perhaps by which she feels professionally compromised. The ethics of the situation—how I went about writing the paper and how I engaged with her during the course of our exchange—do not trouble me. But the moral dimension is another issue. To put it bluntly, what right have I to present for public consumption a representation of someone else, particularly where the escape hatch of interpretive play and the indeterminacy of "truth" cannot sufficiently address crucial questions of appropriation and perhaps the transgression of basic tenets of human consideration?

The narratives of many autobiographers repeatedly and openly acknowledge the role of subjective interpretation and selective memory. The poet David Mura, for instance, closes his memoir *Where the Body Meets Memory* by noting, "The more I tell the stories, the falser they get. That's because I see more complications, not less; other layers crop up, unexpected voices. My view isn't the final one, even if here I get the last say." Writer bell hooks places her autobiographical narrative *Bone Black* in the gap between often mutually exclusive terms, calling it "an unconventional memoir. . . . This is autobiography as truth and myth—as poetic witness." While such caveats do not, to my mind, at all negate the value of the autobiographical enterprise, neither do they give me a clue as to how I might begin to say something about the problems, and responsibilities, of progressive and experimental scholarship in relation to subjects who are neither. Much feminist inquiry and scholarship by people of color critically questions its own motives and occlusions—an impulse I share—but isn't this in some ways the search for a guilt-free space, as though one could write oneself into a pure space of innocence? Is this gesture both an acknowledgment and a disavowal of the power of narrative?

Finally, in asserting that Althea is not a "good subject," I implicitly present myself as precisely that. But on what scale can I make that claim? Narrative authority? Authorial prerogative? Friends and colleagues have suggested that I am under no obligation to employ a pseudonym, that it is not my responsibility to protect Althea within a narrative that, after all, is mine. But if this all isn't quite about rights understood legalistically, surely we cannot simply evacuate questions of rightness. If we cannot speak about Truth, we must neverthe-less ask difficult questions about the truth-value underpinning our forays into autobiographically based theorizing—because the answers, or partial answers, we come to may help us nego-tiate a path that leads us away from righteous cleaving to a single story; caveat-laden, self-reflexive doubt; guilty fictions; and silence.

Bionic Child

Lisa Drostova

Summer 1976

Detroit radiates like a griddle. The heat slides into everything, every crevice, even between the roots of my hair, and settles. We've just emerged from the cool, dim, three-storied confines of the house my parents are thinking about buying on Seyburn Street so we can escape Mason, a rural town outside a suburb of the state capital. The kind of place where getting another stoplight generates a lot of hoopla. Mason boasts exactly one black family, and one Jewish one, namely mine. "If both our families are at an event," my supremely urban parents joke, "you know they're letting everyone in." It's a joke with an edge. My cosmopolitan mother is slowly going insane in Mason.

The house is in West Village, a gracious if shabby old neighborhood near the Detroit River that's getting a little peely around the edges. It's about an hour and a half from Detroit to Mason, so we head to the McDonald's on Jefferson for lunch before hitting the road. Jefferson is a wide boulevard that curves along the river, finally debouching into the broad lawns and old money of Grosse Pointe. East of downtown, large, stately red-brick apartment buildings from the 1920s and '30s cling to the water. As we wait in line to order our hamburgers, I notice something odd.

"And then," my mother says when she tells this story, "in your clear, high-pitched voice, you asked, 'Why are there so many black people in here?' I was horrified and hoped nobody had heard you. But they had. People were turning around to look."

The moment is still vivid to me: I stand there between my sweating parents, each of them holding one of my hands. The view is all bright orange laminate counter and dark brown knees below white shorts. My father clears his throat and looks thoughtful.

"Well, kiddo," he says in his laid-back voice, "it has a lot to do with the Industrial Revolution, which started in England a couple of hundred years ago."

Two hours later, back in Mason, our lunch paid for, eaten, and largely forgotten, my father wraps up his explanation of how economic forces led to the enslavement of Africans. He's touched on the Middle Passage, the Underground Railroad, and the "white flight" from the city to the suburbs that emptied out so many beautiful Detroit houses. I know about the mills, the labor movement, the northward migration of African Americans looking for work, the invaluable contributions of African Americans to every area of endeavor.

I am six years old.

Ever since then, whenever someone in the family is winding up to give a long answer to a simple question, we joke to each other, "Don't give me the Industrial Revolution. Give me the *short* answer."

It's the Fourth of July that same year. We haven't moved yet. I'm at a picnic in the park in Mason, spitting watermelon seeds through the gap between my front teeth and running around with the other children. The best part of the playground is a yellow fiberglass tube large enough for a few kids to sit inside. Inside the tube, the light is the exact same color as the cover of *My Mother the Mail Carrier/Mi Mama la Cartera,* a bilingual book about a little Latina girl who lives with her single mother. I have a collection of children's books about strong women (or females of one species or another, such as the headstrong, curious penguin, Carlotta, who rescues an injured scientist out on the ice when she's supposed to be fishing with the other mama penguins). My mother has seen to it. For gifts, my parents give me trucks instead of Barbies, and I own exactly one dress (also non-gender-specific yellow, and long enough to cover my scabby knees), which I only wear to fancy events. Sometimes I feel like an experiment my parents are conducting. I am the Bionic Child, built to be unhampered by sexist or racist conditioning. They buy weird books from feminist presses. They make a point of introducing me to all sorts of people, and they try to make sense of history for me. I am forbidden to use words like "nigger" and "kike," even though I hear them frequently outside the house. Like the Six Million Dollar Man or the Bionic Woman, I've been modified; like them, you can't tell from the outside what I am on the inside. My parents cross their fingers and wait to see what happens.

This year, because of the bicentennial, the school has picked a *Mayflower* theme for its summer reading program. Each student has been given a sheet of paper printed with a cartoon of several children dressed as Pilgrims in feathered hats. Every time we finish a book, we get another sticker to put over one of the hats. The children in the drawing are black and white and Asian and Native American. They don't look like the kids in my town, all of whom are white and Christian.

The three years we've lived here have been a strain on my mother, who grew up on Chicago's south side and is accustomed to a little more activity, a little more diversity. There, she volunteered for Reverend Jesse Jackson and went home to a neighborhood full of Jews and Italians and African Americans. Here in Mason, she keeps house, works part-time as a rural-route mail carrier, and tries to stay calm when I come home crying because the neighbor kids have teased me for being Jewish. "Why didn't you tell me I have horns?" I've blubbered, rubbing my scalp through my hair. I've felt around for what I imagine must be the nubbins like those on the heads of baby goats. It hasn't occurred to me that my parents don't have horns. Maybe they have to saw them off occasionally, or trim them. Maybe that's what they're doing those weekend mornings when their bedroom door is locked. "We have to get out of here," my mother tells my father. "We can't raise a child here."

The summer of the bicentennial of the United States' independence from Britain, I have one brilliant day of running around with other kids and not thinking about my horns. Otherwise, I keep to myself and read enough books to cover all the hats with stickers. I start affixing the extra stickers around the edges of the sheet. My parents keep looking for a house in Detroit.

Eric is long and lean and slouches a little to make himself less intimidating. He lives with his girlfriend across the street and down a few houses from our new place. At their parties, they do artsy things like smoke hand-rolled cigarettes and project Jean Cocteau's version of *Beauty and the Beast* on a roll-up screen. I see the film *Powers of Ten* for the first time at their house, long before I see it at school. Eric is our favorite neighbor, more than the people directly across the street with the two sons my age, or the two ancient sisters and their brother next door, all pinched and powdery. Eric is *hip*.

My father's parents live with us in our new place in Detroit for a few years. While my grandfather is content to sit in the living room reading biographies, my grandmother is far more energetic, a tornado of dubious Irishness and Chanel No. 5. I am secretly proud that when she breaks her elbow, she doesn't do it in some grandmotherly way involving stairs or bathtub or kitchen—she does it disco dancing with the much-younger Eric. This makes her almost impossibly cool in my book.

My grandmother, who bakes a million kinds of cookies and gleefully uses old-fashioned words like "addlepated" and "dingbat," is the Bionic Grandma.

Summer 1978

The Seyburn house is on the corner of the block. It is broken into with such depressing frequency that my parents drive through the alley behind the house whenever they come home, to make sure we aren't being burgled. One night, my mother and I are on our usual patrol in her massive silver-gray Chrysler Cordoba when, as we turn the corner, we see that the back gate and back door stand wide open. All the lights are on in the house, and our things are strewn across the backyard. My mother curses and drives around the block to drop me off at the next-door neighbor's house to call the police.

Over at the neighbor's, I have no idea that my mother has driven back around our house just in time to pin one of the burglars—and our television—up against the garage. I stand at the window that faces the side of our house and watch as two strangers casually move back and forth through the kitchen and dining room, picking things up to examine them. Then a third comes running through, and his friends follow. They go out the front door, more or less straight into the densely muscled arms of Tamara, the cop who just pulled up in her squad car. Bad guys tucked safely away, Tamara and her partner take our statements.

The part of the story that my mother still loves—and there isn't much to love, considering that we later learn the perpetrators are on parole for murder committed during a burglary—is that when the police ask me to identify the race of the men I saw through the windows, I hesitate. My mother believes it's because she and my father have done such a good job raising me to be colorblind. I don't know. Perhaps I know perfectly well the men are African American, but I don't want to say so for fear of seeming racist, even when it comes to a simple statement of fact—there were black men I don't recognize in my house—especially since the officer asking the question is black. Eventually I say, "They had afros, so they must have been black." My mother views my hesitation as a triumph.

✄

It's the Fourth of July after the break-in. The burglars took everything, down to my mother's black velvet opera cloak and my father's suits. What they didn't manage to get away from the house before we got there is largely ruined, between being dropped in panic or covered with fingerprint powder. So my parents and I are at Highland Appliance, looking for a new television to replace the one still in the police evidence locker. We seem to do this often. But it's not always during the Fourth of July sale or during the height of summer. It's dark outside, and humid; it's brightly lit in the warehouse, and humid. Besides the washers and dryers and ovens, there are rows of televisions as far as the eye can see, big ones, small ones, all turned on, all broadcasting in slightly different colors. Bored witless, I've wandered away from my parents.

We are the only white people in the store. Although more than half of my classmates are black, I'm not accustomed to being around so many black *adults,* and I'm pretty uncomfortable. I'm also still pretty scared, post-break-in, of black men. I feel like we're in the wrong place somehow, like the other people in the store are looking at us and wondering what we're doing here. Aren't we supposed to be up in Birmingham or Bloomfield Hills or even Royal Oak, where the other white people are? In my drama class a few months before, our teacher took a Method approach to teaching us how to act. "Imagine that you are heavy, sticky, and totally limp," she told me when I played the tar baby in an Uncle Remus skit. Brer Rabbit and Brer Bear fought over me; I clung to whichever one had a hand on me and thought, "I am covered in tar. I am heavy, sticky, and limp. Heavy, sticky, and limp."

In Highland Appliance, I decide to try out what I've learned in our little foray into acting. "I belong here," I think to myself. "I am big and cool and unafraid. I am not like those frightened white people who live in the suburbs. I am not really white at all."

A black man standing at the next television over is laughing at a newscaster's stupid joke. We smile at each other and suddenly I'm comfortable; I no longer feel everyone's eyes crawling on me. I feel bigger, and welcome. When my parents find me to tell me it's time to leave, I sulk.

My parents send me to a Quaker grade school whose student population mirrors that of the city, 60/40 black/white. The most earnest teachers imaginable staff Detroit Friends. Every year we sullenly sit through the movie *Gentle Persuasion*, about Quakers refusing to fight in some war or another, and we're taught that racism is violence. I am one of two Jews in my class, a novelty, called upon to explain Hanukkah and Passover. We know the names of all the countries in Africa better than we do those in Europe. We go on a field trip to see a play about Harriet Tubman. Our teachers are determined to redress the slave ships, the plantations, the trackers with dogs. Frederick Douglass, Dr. King, and George Washington Carver are our heroes. We tease each other cruelly about clothes and athletic ability and smarts, but never, ever, about our skin color.

Despite ourselves, we are Bionic Children.

Elbee, whom everyone calls Elbeano. Awkward and terribly sweet. Thick glasses, a nasal voice, a stutter that makes him even shyer. I don't know what becomes of him. I still think of him often. I hope he's incredibly successful. I hope he showed them all.

Al, chunky, calm. Explains that Adidas stands for All Day I Dream About Sex. Al is the first boy willing to let me play Kill the Man with the Ball outside after school with the others, a game that consists of piles of boys with arms and legs sticking out. He's also the first to yell encouragement when I prove, amazingly, to be a good runner and a better tackle. He gets hit by a car walking home from a friend's house the night the Tigers win the World Series in '84.

Articulate, voluble Winston. Born with a hole in his heart that he talks about during art class. One day he brings some cow's eyes to science class—his mother has bought a whole cow head to cook—and the boys and I gleefully dissect them while the other girls shiver and complain and cling to the wall. Winston is one of the truly nicest people I will ever meet, perhaps because he suspects his life will be too short to waste time being mean.

Tracy, Cassandra's daughter. Much longer and skinnier than I am, so her hand-me-downs fit me very strangely. At her house, we listen to the Jackson Five and talk about how cute Michael is.

Jamal, in the oversized glasses and tight designer jeans, who regularly slams my locker door shut on my fingers. "It's because he likes you," says my mother. In fifth grade, he accidentally-on-purpose hits me in the arm with a baseball bat one afternoon when the sub has disappeared to cry in the faculty lounge, and my mother is called. In the too-familiar Children's Hospital ER waiting room, I muse on her theory that he likes me. Probably not, I think.

Natasha, elegant and commanding, the hub around which the wheel of popular girls spins. Her dad is black, her mother white; they own a flower shop. Natasha is always neatly groomed and wearing fashionable clothing. She knows which music is hot and which dorky, and years later, every time I hear the disco hit "Ring My Bell," I will think of her. At her tenth birthday party, in a rare moment of not making fun of my too-short double-knit polyester pants, she chooses my freak dancing as the best in a contest, and I receive a tub of green goo as a prize. The green goo I lose almost immediately. The glow of finally, astonishingly, being good at something Natasha values will cling to me for twenty years, following me into West African dance and belly dance classes, where I will still hear her voice explaining, "Freaking is easy. You just shake your butt and boobs, a lot." Nobody is surprised when she grows up to be a fashion model and the wife of a hunky professional basketball player.

Collis, who spends lunch hours in the science classroom with Marc and me, screwing around because the teacher likes us and thinks we're doing real experiments. She's not there the day we call our experiment Pour Rubbing Alcohol All Over a Lab Table and Set It on Fire. Only my insistence that we all wear lab goggles ensures that Collis and Marc retain their eyebrows (I stand as far away as possible). We are the Three Musketeers. Years later, Collis will claim that he was secretly imprisoned by the Feds for hacking into the NSA computer system. Yet more years later, when I Google him and nothing comes up, I'll wonder if he really did get spirited away by the government.

Shannon, who lives with his grandmother. We get assigned to do a project on human anatomy together and choose the female reproductive system. I do the research, write the paper, and cast a partial torso by wrapping my own flat hips in plaster bandages. Inside, on wires, hang organs I make from papier-mâché. I'm never clear on just what Shannon contributes, but he's so charismatic I don't care. Much.

Where did you all go? Everything I learned about how cool it was to be black, I learned from you. I still miss you guys. I'm sorry I lost contact after I switched schools and was suddenly and bizarrely surrounded by white kids whose language and culture I struggled to understand. I often felt as though I had betrayed you somehow, moving out to a suburban school.

Well, Jamal, maybe I don't miss you all that much. My fingers sure don't.

We do not, in my family, consider ourselves exactly white. This is not uncommon for Jews, especially those who remember that when we first came to this country, we were often called black. My mother tells me that I'm darker than all the white kids I know, which is probably not true (darker than Kristin and Anouk, sure, but Michael Buist? The Levin girls?). But I never call her on it. "White" in my mind comes to stand for a very narrow range of color, maybe from typing paper to eggnog, and a clearly defined range of behavior. White people are blond and blue-eyed, with little pointy noses. They like things like Jell-O and meatloaf and casseroles made with cream of mushroom soup as a base. They virtually own Thanksgiving and Christmas. They're uptight.

We, on the other hand, are sort of yellowish or greenish, depending on the season. We have dark brown hair and eyes, and big proud noses. Occasionally Mom makes her favorite treat by frying onions in chicken fat until they turn black and crispy, which disgusts me, and once a year at Passover, the first course is gefilte fish, which also disgusts me. Being Jewish confuses the color equation: You can look white, but not be it; white is a manifestation not only of skin color (my dream boy Matt Schenk, from our congregation, is as blond and blue a cream puff as you can imagine) and culture, but of history. We weren't here for that whole *Mayflower* party, we say, running around in the feathered hats, handing out the smallpox blankets. And we got here after that whole terrible slavery business; that wasn't us. We invoke images of our relatives, as thoroughly wrapped as stuffed cabbages in their dark heavy clothes and squinting uncertainly for the camera. We're strangers here ourselves, we say. Remember that we weren't too well loved at first either. We do our best to deflect everything, true or not, that is negative about whiteness. My mother in particular has always been insistent that we are not white in the commonly understood sense of the word.

But neither are we black, in the commonly understood sense of that word. We can shed our Ellis Island headscarves and slide undetected through the land of blond casserole eaters. I learn this when my folks move me into a more academically challenging school after sixth grade. In the new school, I have to work harder for good grades, but that's not what makes the transition from an urban Quaker school to a private suburban one a little rocky. "What are all these white people doing here?" I find myself wondering in the first few weeks. When I say "auntie" instead of "aunt," I get in trouble and my parents get a phone call. When I check the "Other" box for race on my standardized test form, I get in trouble and my parents get a phone call. My new friends aren't allowed to come over after school because their parents are afraid to let their kids go downtown. In eighth grade, the one sleepover I host requires a virtual blizzard of phone calls. My friends' parents seem to envision Detroit as a howling post-apocalyptic wasteland populated by roving bands of armed black marauders hell-bent on defiling white children, or at the very least covering them with germs and giving them diseases.

It is very clear, although it is seldom spoken, that these adults are afraid of my black friends and neighbors and former classmates: Eric and Officer Tamara and the guy in the appliance store, Elbee and Natasha and Jamal. I'm too young yet to see that they don't mean anything by it, that they just haven't thought it through. Happily, it doesn't seem to touch my friends, other than what I see as a little needless fear. I don't think much of their parents, but I go to their suburban houses and eat their spiceless, chicken-fat-and-onion-free casseroles and their Jell-O. It's the only way I can socialize. I'm flying under false colors, but which ones? I feel like a spy, but for whom?

꙼

As a kid, I had the impression that black people were inherently a lot cooler than white people. They knew what was going on. They were more stylish, more self-assured, hipper; their music was the real thing, and the validity of their fashion sense was unquestionable. But more than that, they were *real*. They had suffered and persevered. They thumbed their noses at the devil, with their generous picnics and bright clothes and easy laughter. Although our experiences were different, on some level they must have reminded me of my own folk, who had survived the Diaspora and the pogroms and the death camps and were still joyous. A joke my mother emailed me, "How to explain Jewish holidays to Gentiles," seemed to apply equally to African Americans: "They tried to kill us, we survived, let's eat!" While I understood rationally that American blacks had been through the wringer, they seemed to be having an awfully good time, and they moved through the world with more assurance than I.

I also thought they held a tremendous amount of power, but a friend my age who grew up in San Francisco tells me I was hoodwinked. "You had no idea what was really going on. In the '70s, the conditions for African Americans were terrible." But I don't remember it that way. There were black people in my picture books, in my school, on television, in government. When I was a kid, it felt to me like we were getting somewhere, like blacks and whites were well on their way to peaceful coexistence. Everyone I knew believed that black slavery was a terrible stain on American history that decent people would do everything to try to fix so we could move on. Until I went off to a suburban high school, I thought we were all on the same page. And these days, there seems to be so much more tension that sometimes it feels like the world is conspiring to overturn my parents' experiment, to dash the beakers and burners to the floor, to leave the lab a smoking ruin.

I wonder if I remember things differently than they were.

I try to hold on to an endless Fourth of July. Eric and my grandmother and my parents. My schoolmates, Winston and Elbee and Natasha, Anouk and Kristin and Michael, are all alive and wearing jeans with huge bell-bottoms and embroidered peasant tops. We're talking about art and community. We're surrounded by our laughing, multihued families. We work at what we love. And while we never forget that we have been scattered and persecuted and enslaved in the past, we remain facing ever forward, our hands out to each other. We see the colors of our various skins as beauty, not destiny. We know there's more inside than will ever be visible on the outside.

We are bionic.

Black Men

Faith Adiele

Falling

When I was five years old, I tripped on a throw rug in my baby sitter's house and hurtled face forward onto the coffee table, an immense slab of petrified California redwood. Quick as it happened, the arc of my fall segmented itself, colors separating in a kaleidoscope, and crystallized in my memory: the rug sucking at my ankles, the giddy lurch across the floor, the crest through the air, weightless, my jangling heart, disbelief as I spied the waiting block—solid, glistening.

I was already screaming when my nose smacked the table. Over the noise, I heard a crack like the cut that severs a tree, saw the brown spine of a Douglas fir submitting to my grandfather's ax.

The baby sitter, who'd been in the kitchen coating slices of Wonder Bread with thick swirls of margarine and dousing them with sugar (an after-school snack I adored, much to my mother's horror), came tearing down the hall.

"What happened?" she shouted, the sugar shaker still clutched in her fist.

I couldn't respond. Pain vibrated through cartilage into the roots of my teeth. I crumpled to the floor, clutching my face.

She yanked my quivering hands away to check for fracture, her fingers leaving a gritty trail of sugar across my cheeks. Then, though not a particularly demonstrative woman, she lifted me into the large recliner and locked her arms around me.

"Go 'way!" I shrieked at the other children who, wide-eyed and solemn, ringed the recliner, some wailing helpfully, others tugging the baby sitter's apron, wanting to know, "Why she crying?"

I howled and howled. More than the pain itself, I remember the taste of sugar mixed with tears leaking into my mouth, salt and sweet, the flavor of amazement, amazement to learn that yes, life was this, too. I don't remember the trip to the ER, the arrival of my mother, the painkillers, the days and nights of ice packs.

By some miracle, my nose wasn't broken. "I fell," I announced proudly to strangers, and in 1968, people believed me, could still believe in children, even brown ones, falling. Over the next few days, a thick root of blood spread out beneath the golden surface of my cheeks, staining them the color of bruised plums. The bridge of my nose puffed and held. For nearly six months, I resembled a raccoon—curious, slightly anxious, with crusty purple skin ringing my eyes.

ぐぶつ

One of my favorite photographs was taken a few months later. Michael-Vaino, a.k.a. Uncle Mike, and a friend were dancing in my grandparents' living room in cowboy hats. Uncle Mike, his pale Finn eyes droopy, snapped the fingers of one hand, wobbled a bottle of gin in the other. His friend, a Swede like Old Pappa, my lumberman grandfather, balanced me on his hip.

My mother had been playing Nigerian Highlife LPs on the stereo, and Uncle Mike's friend, drawn by the hypnotic twang of the talking drum speaking to the guitar, like someone calling your name underwater, popped his head into the room. "Hey, what's this music?"

"Yeah, cool." Uncle Mike followed behind, drawing the string of his flat-brimmed hat tight. Ever since childhood, he'd dressed like a cowboy in an old black-and-white movie.

My mother stared pointedly at his hand and shook her head.

"I know, I know." He gave the bottle a fluid twist of the wrist, a cowboy spinning his pistols before reholstering. "It's only for a second. We're on our way out."

The Highlife swelled, spurred by the singer's admonition that *Everybody dey party,* and my uncle's friend swept me into his arms, saying. "Hear that? Everybody party, something-something."

My mother hesitated a moment, then smiled. Extending her arms before her like a hula dancer, crooked at the elbows, she swiveled her hips to the slower underbeat, the way my Nigerian father had taught her before he left. Like a grass skirt, her brown ponytail swayed from side to side.

Uncle Mike snapped his fingers, shuffled his feet across the carpet, sang "something-something" in my ear. Despite the fact that it was his friend who held me, his friend who told me how pretty I was (something Uncle Mike had never said, either before or after my raccoon rings), my uncle was the one I loved.

My mother ended it.

"Look goofy!" she called, framing us in the lens of her Brownie camera. "In other words, just be yourselves." The flash bleached the room, breaking the spell.

Uncle Mike checked his watch and jerked his head toward the door. Outside, the crunch of gravel signaled that the others were assembling in the driveway. Whenever his pack of loud, good-natured friends came by in their well-ironed jeans, they left their bottles outside in fast cars with deep bucket seats and carried me on their shoulders, recounting their latest motorbike triumphs.

The friend spun me one last time and released. "Thank you, madam." He bowed.

"Don't go," I begged.

Uncle Mike doffed his hat and flattened it onto my head with two pats. "'Night, cowpoke." Then he was gone. I listened hard in his wake: gravel flying, welcome shouts, car doors opening to blasts of squealing electric guitar and shuddering bass, metallic slams and revved motors. The music of my disappeared-to-Africa father couldn't compete.

Most nights Uncle Mike came home after I was in bed. Most days he slept past noon. Awake, he was often grumpy. His jovial moments were brief, always halfway out the door.

Baby Vaino, the One Left Behind

I come from a long line of unlucky men, men who disappeared to unsettled countries, to civil-war-torn countries, to mental institutions, to the barn with a bottle of vodka. Men in our family couldn't quite manage to stay home. They wandered—restless, driven by gold, war, emotion—and rarely returned, despite the best intentions. Growing up on the family farm, I inherited the understanding that men were fragile, prone to leaving us behind.

Who's to blame? Let's start with country—Finland, with its brooding soundtrack by Sibelius and its tight-lipped, hard-drinking citizens. I blame the flat, icy landscape with its meager sunlight and long winter days. I blame history—Sweden and Russia leaning like the long shadow of death, recurring conquests interspersed with ill-fated stoic resistance. Or shall I blame hunger and displacement, the generic lot of the immigrant?

But why is it each generation assumed history and landscape were things only women could survive? For that I blame twin legacies—names and lies: All the men in our family are named after Baby Vaino, the One Left Behind. His abandonment was the original lie.

In 1889, my great-grandfather the Cursed was born in Finland, the second of three sons. When he was still young, his father snatched him and his older brother out of the shade of Russia and fled to the United States. His mother remained behind with Vaino, the baby. Father and sons settled in Ashtabula, Ohio, a bustling port city on Lake Erie, where the father found work as a carpenter.

When I was nine and much enamored of slave narratives, I thrilled to learn that fifty years before my ancestors' arrival, the Ashtabula River had been a stop on the Underground Railroad for slaves fleeing to Canada. I studied how runaways walked for miles in the dark, running their blistered hands up the sides of trees to feel for the north-facing moss, how conductors placed burning candles in station windows, much like the ones we lit in December for the *tonttu*, farm sprites. My heart throbbed with justice and injustice. Despite a Nigerian and Nordic heritage, I longed to claim black Americans like John Park, who ferried hundreds of fellow slaves across the Ohio River.

I had to settle for the Hubbards, a white family who owned a successful lumberyard and belonged to Ashtabula's antislavery society. William Hubbard built a large, white-pillared house near the lake, where nearly every night passengers slipped into cubbyholes in the cellar and hayloft, their last stop before freedom. The white man who likely employed my Finnish ancestors was as close as I came to slave resistance.

I imagined my great-grandfather the Cursed in his dark woolens and heavy boots clomping in late from Hubbard's lumberyard, unaware of the legacy of black slaves above his head, beneath his feet.

When his mother and Baby Vaino, the One Left Behind, died back in Finland, his father remarried and fathered three more children.

Handicaps

Michael-Vaino, a.k.a. Uncle Mike, is handicapped.

I am six, and we have moved to my grandparents' farm. This means two things: One, my mother and Old Pappa have reconciled, and two, my interest in family gossip is born. The sound of dropping voices, as my mother and Mummi start to whisper, is my sign to creep into hiding.

Handicapped! I freeze in the hallway. It sounds bad, like being retarded. Like giant Mark Kludas two doors down, who smells and weeps like an angry baby whenever the neighborhood kids rile him. Uncle Mike, who wears tight jeans and races motocross, is nothing like Mark.

Nonetheless, being handicapped is why he isn't able to go to Vietnam. This is also confusing. I've been in more protests than I can count, bearded graduate students passing me from shoulder to shoulder and singing folksongs Mom taught me on her Autoharp, so that he and his friends don't have to go. Uncle Mike will be the one who doesn't disappear. Why, then, should he be disappointed?

"*Shhh,*" my grandmother warns my mother. Uncle Mike is self-conscious about his handicap.

When Uncle Mike finally awakens at three, I am stationed outside his door, trying not to stare. He grunts and staggers to the bathroom. Hearing the door, Mummi darts into his bedroom with a stack of freshly ironed clothes and grabs as many things as she can carry off the floor.

When Uncle Mike emerges in his white terrycloth robe, the bathroom mirror steamed up and his shaggy blond hair combed wet over his ears, I am waiting. He gives me a puzzled glance. I tilt my chin and pretend to study the embroidered hanging above the laundry hamper. Shaking his head, he saunters to the kitchen. I follow, close on his heels.

When he lifts me onto a stool, I scan his face, searching for the handicap. I see Uncle Mike: round, ruddy face, my mother's blue, hound-dog eyes, dashing blond mustache that droops a bit on the left beneath a slightly flattened nose.

Disappointed at the handicap's reluctance to show itself, I frown and demand to know what he's making.

He ignores me, his head burrowed in the refrigerator. Seconds later he emerges, arms loaded. Movements smooth and sure, no evidence of a handicap, he builds a giant sandwich out of leftovers, cottage cheese, fried eggs, and ketchup.

"What next?" I ask at each step, trembling with horror.

He snorts an occasional answer: Meatloaf. Pickles. He loads the finished sandwich onto a baking sheet and shoves it into the oven. My stomach recoils.

"You know," he says, looking up from sawing at the bubbling sandwich, suddenly talkative, "I heard that President Nixon puts ketchup on his cottage cheese." He grins. "He must be the only other person besides me!"

And though I know we aren't supposed to like President Nixon, I giggle.

Great-Grandpa the Cursed

Sometime during the immigrant wave of the 1890s, my great-great-grandfather and his two elder sons came to Ohio, and as was customary in chain immigration, his wife and newborn remained in Finland. When they died, my great-great-grandfather remarried and fathered three more children.

"Actually," my grandmother confesses, "they didn't die. My grandmother and Baby Vaino lived on in Finland for years."

Stunned, I watch her hands, smelling of yeast and rye, as she kneads the *limpa*. At age ten, I'm obsessed with family stories and photos. I can't imagine what compelled a father to tell his sons that their mother and brother had died. Was it his plan from the start to abandon his wife and construct a new life on the blank page of America?

Mummi shakes her head, working the brown dough with strong fingers. She doesn't know. Her father, my cursed great-grandfather, died of stomach ulcers when she was a baby. The story came secondhand to her.

I imagine that this event—the loss of his mother and baby brother, his father's lie—is the moment my great-grandfather became cursed. I know how he feels. We two are alike, caught in between, with one foot, one parent in the New World, one still in the Old. Two years after my birth, without ever having seen me, my father disappeared to deepest, darkest Africa, never to be seen again. Like so many of those who invented America, my great-grandfather emerged from the dream of migration only partly intact. Half of himself he carried, never waking, forever out of reach.

I study Mummi's face, her nose like a soft, drooping beak, and try to imagine her cursed father as a boy. I see a sleepwalker. A dark boy with light eyes, he stumbles through a house with hidden rooms beneath the stairs, behind the fireplace, blind to his American stepmother and new siblings. He tries to recall his mother's face, tries to imagine Baby Vaino, the One Left Behind, now grown to a boy. He lies awake nights, troubled by the voices of former slaves praying beneath the floorboards. Like them, he will rest in this place only momentarily. He wonders if he'll ever see his mother and brother again, fears they await a summons that will never come.

Bad Habits

Michael-Vaino, a.k.a. Uncle Mike, is in trouble.

From my hiding place in the hall linen closet, I hear Mummi stirring her tea, teaspoon tinkling.

"He just has Bad Habits," my mother says.

Like not taking out the trash? Or watching too much TV, which rots your noodle?

Uncle Mike didn't come home last night. Wherever he was, Old Pappa wanted him to stay there overnight "to learn his lesson." My mother chuckles. "Dinner tonight should be fun." A metal chair leg scrapes across the linoleum. "Let me call the Funks to see if Faith can eat there."

Foiled, I steam in the closet. I am the only child among adults. If I am six, Uncle Mike is twenty-two, the family member closest to me in age.

I insist on taking my naps in his room. Except for the same heavy Scandinavian furniture that looks as if it's been shellacked in honey, his bedroom differs from the rest of the house. His shelves are crammed with tall, sparkly racing trophies. Two doors in the bed's golden headboard slide back to reveal tiny packets of tissue-thin paper called "zigzag" and tall glass tubes of stinky water. I am convinced these have some-thing to do with Uncle Mike's Bad Habits. Back issues of *Playboy* and *Penthouse* rise in the closet. Fending off sleep, I read voraciously, dazed by mounds of breasts like the pale mountains surrounding our valley home.

Rivers

In the 1890s, one adult male and two male children, all named Hautajoki, left Finland for America. My great-great-grand-mother nodded grimly from the misty banks of the Hauta River, their namesake. The newborn balanced on her hip, she watched her husband and sons go. This was their agreement. He would take the two elder sons; she would remain behind with Baby Vaino. The Lutheran Church banned divorce, but couldn't control for the vicissitudes of immigration.

Father and sons settled in Ashtabula, where there was carpentry work and a thriving Finnish community. After some time, Great-great-grandpa Hautajoki took a wife. The Hautajoki thus cleaved in two, one stream on the mother-land, the other a tributary flowing in America. In time, it split again. The branch from which I am descended turned out to be perpetually sickly, as if we never quite recovered from the wound.

On November 11, 1908, the cursed middle son left his father's house to marry another Finnish immigrant. He was nineteen. Like his father, he became a carpenter and fathered three children: Tati Rauha, the eldest; my grandmother, the baby; and a son. He named the son Vaino-Johan, after his younger and older brothers.

Even as a child, I knew he had erred in naming. For a time, however, things were good. Husband and wife lived in a comfortable house that he built, and food was plentiful.

There is only one photograph of my great-grandfather the Cursed. In 1911, the family sat for a formal studio portrait: husband, wife, and the two elder children; my grandmother was not yet born.

Tati Rauha, large bow atop her pale curls, stands on a table, her hand pressed for leverage to her mother's breast. Holding her bottom lip between her teeth, she clutches her brother's hand.

Great-grandpa the Cursed, well-groomed in a dark suit, also holds Vaino-Johan. The two of them, with their wide, angular jaws and olive skin, couldn't look more different from the women.

An odd distortion breaks the sharp sepia image, a smear or blur in the upper right-hand corner throwing Great-grandpa's head out of focus. Already, three or four years before his death at age twenty-six from stomach ulcers, he is receding from his family, becoming indistinct.

As if she senses this, Tati Rauha clenches her brother's hand, seemingly determined to wrest Vaino-Johan from their cursed father's grasp and keep him safe in the world with her—a role she and my grandmother played, with only limited success, all his life.

Gifts

Presents from Michael-Vaino, a.k.a. Uncle Mike, are always worth the wait. Despite this, as each birthday and Joulu approach, I see my mother watching him, worried, wondering if he will make it on time, or even remember.

There is the Frosty the Snowman Snow Cone Maker, which, though it requires hours of hard scraping to make a single snow cone, is exactly like the one I admired on television. There is a battery-powered pottery wheel that sprays mud everywhere.

One Joulu, he builds a three-story dollhouse from my mother's design with real tile and Formica floors from factory remnants at work. He is so exhausted from all the late nights that he snores through Christmas dinner.

The Joulu I enter junior high, he hands me a heavy tan-and-brown envelope. Having recently discovered clothes, I instantly recognize the logo for Nordstrom's, a department store in Seattle, and say a little prayer, *Please let it be a lot, like twenty-five dollars,* before ripping it open.

A certificate for fifty dollars—more money than I have ever seen—slips into my trembling fingers. After he drags my arms from around his neck, I spend the rest of the evening glowing and shy.

"Half that amount would've been generous," my mother marvels later as they sit in the darkened living room sipping *glögi*. From my perch in the laundry room, I can see the colored lights blinking on the tree.

Uncle Mike chuckles. "Well, in fact, I only intended to spend twenty-five, but . . ." his voice drops, conspiratorial, "the guy in front of me spent forty dollars, and the saleswoman was uh, you know, pretty foxy."

My mother laughs. "Praise God for the male ego!"

I slump against the cold washing machine, careful not to make any noise. Junior high will be full of moments like this, the adult in me recognizing humor and the child wanting to cry. For one entire evening, I'd thought that his love finally matched mine. That I was worth twice as much.

Three decades after her father's death, sometime between the end of World War II and 1958, when she started keeping a diary, my grandmother discovered that her father the Cursed had not died of stomach ulcers in 1915. In fact, he had not died at all.

She tells me the story when I'm eleven, sitting on my kitchen stool watching the *limpa* turn dark brown through the little yellowed window in the oven door.

One day, by some miracle of mail forwarding, a letter arrived all the way from Ohio from the director of a sanatorium, who regretted to inform the Hautajoki family that he had just expired.

Like milk left on the shelf too long.

Mummi pulls the *limpa* from the oven, heavy and dark. An acrid wave of rye floods the kitchen. Thirty years later, her dead father had died again, his life flickering across her cornea for only an instant.

I'm full of questions. How did her mother carry so many secrets to her grave? That her husband had been alive all this time, insane, institutionalized for more than half his life. That all this time, his children had been carrying this gene unawares. What, who, where?

Mummi cuts the *limpa,* holding the sharp knife in soft hands, her voice low. She doesn't say how it felt to learn the news about her father in her thirties, once it was too late to do anything. I know she worried about her son, Michael-Vaino, a.k.a. Uncle Mike.

Whatever her feelings, she does not voice them, does not commit them to her diary, does not change the family register at the back of the album. Great-grandpa the Cursed remains dead at age twenty-six of stomach ulcers. This is an oral story, passed from her to my mother and me.

Rivers

After my great-grandfather the Cursed's institutionalization, the family was always poor. For the next ten years, his wife and three children lived like nomads, moving from state to state on the immigrant circuit, chasing rumors of work. There is no family account of what happened to the other Hautajoki men, father and older brother of the Cursed. Supposedly the new American stepmother discouraged close relations. There is no explanation for the older brother's disappearance, another split in the river.

Bad Genes

Later I lug the encyclopedia up to the roof and pore over entries on schizophrenia and depression, studying them as carefully as photos in the family album. I'm convinced that I, too, am insane. I wonder how to break the news to my mother. I am prone to fits of disordered thinking. Extreme sadness. Exaggerated gaiety. Blame Finland.

Looking out on fields of mint, I weep a bit for Great-grandpa the Cursed, my oft abandoned, lied to, and lied about forebear. First taken from his childhood home, and then replaced by an American stepmother and three half-siblings, until, haunted by the voices beneath his bed, he was finally abandoned in the middle of a strange and unfriendly country by his young wife.

Then I mist for his wife, left like my mother to raise her children alone. Now I understand why she fled Ohio, taking her children west.

Once the family got as far west as you can go, enter my mother, disowned at nineteen by Old Pappa for "going black," then abandoned for Africa, now trying to be both (white) mother and (black) father to an American child.

"More stories!" I demand, and my grandmother explains that Uncle Mike's mustache droops to hide the white veins where his face is sewn together, where there used to be an open cavity.

I follow her lead, punching the puffy *limpa*, watching it collapse. Born with a cleft palate, ruptured left eardrum, and fused nasal cavity, Michael-Vaino, a.k.a. Uncle Mike, spent his babyhood in hospitals, arms sheathed in cardboard restraints—Mummi holds up her arms, articulating them stiffly at the elbows—so he couldn't pick at his face.

By the time he got out of the hospital, he was timid and cross. He hated speech therapy. He hated change. Every winter, he cried at having to wear long sleeves, and then when summer rolled around, he cried to see his short-sleeved shirts again. Even now he refuses a hearing aid, despite my mother's claim that he can't hear half of what's said. He would rather appear stuck-up than weak. Mummi works the dough methodically, sniffling because *limpa* makes her cry.

"She blames herself," my mother explains later as we cut paper dolls at the kitchen table. "She blames herself for Bad Genes."

My mother arranges a fan of American Revolution costumes across the sunny Formica. "And she's never forgiven herself for leaving him alone in the hospital. The doctors made her go home, but Mike was terrified. He sobbed all night. By morning, the restraints were shredded." Over the years, a series of operations were performed on Uncle Mike's face and ear. Every time he screamed, my grandmother screamed, too. One operation, when he was an adult, entailed systematically shattering his nose and then reconstructing it like an ancient artifact, shard by shard. The procedure was so excruciating that he could only endure part of it and refused to return for the second installment. The left half of his nose remains smashed.

Handicaps

Occasionally, my mother and Michael-Vaino, a.k.a. Uncle Mike, slip into the comfort of childhood. These moments she is once again his sister, not the One Who Got Herself Knocked Up by a Black African, and he is just her brother, not the One Who Is at Best Unreliable and at Worst a Bad Influence on Her Child.

One evening, she follows him into the bathroom and perches on the edge of the bathtub. She's been prattling about Borlaug winning the Nobel Peace Prize—*Yay for farmers!*— but falls silent, watching him shave.

He laughs uneasily. "It's hard to get it even," he apologizes, "with the deformity."

"What're you talking about?"

He shrugs, the blade flashing up the tender flesh of his neck.

She joins him at the mirror, standing on tiptoe, tan cowlicks sprouting like weeds over the hill of his shoulder. "Describe yourself!"

"Go away," he says, resting his elbow atop her head. "You're short, and I'm late."

"I may be short, but I'm tougher than you." She ducks and jabs his ribs. When he doubles over, she grabs his ears. "There," she turns him back to the mirror. "Tell me what you see."

He describes a face split like a mask, a huge, jagged scar and flattened, misshapen nose cleaving the landscape in two. Under the spell of his words, he transforms into an ogre straight out of Norse mythology, the goddess Hel, who haunts me, too. In my grandmother's tales, Hel appears vertically split, half-white, half-black, the black half a putrefying corpse. Though not perhaps the healthiest biracial model for me, she is satisfyingly literal.

My mother gasps. "Sweetie, are you crazy?"

Years later, she will find me weeping before a mirror after my first junior high dance—Big Lips, the only black girl in school, left to hold up the gymnasium walls for two excruciating hours—and ask the same of me.

It seems that leaving the house is a dangerous proposition. Difference announces itself out there, worms its way in. Strangers for whom familiarity doesn't hide handicap see clearly, instantly, who is half-rebuilt and who is half-black. *Hey man, why is your mustache so weird? What are you, deaf? Hey little girl, that white lady can't be your mom; where's your real mom? And why are your lips so big?*

In the unforgiving fluorescence of the bathroom, my mother tries to explain to her brother that his scar and nose are virtually unnoticeable, much as she will try to convince me after the dance that Black is Beautiful, fuck junior high. She speaks desperately, her hands, her cowlicks waving, but it is years too late.

"Yeah, whatever," he says, slapping on Brut cologne like punishment, slipping a flask of something clear into his rear jeans pocket.

Gifts

My mother always knew the truth about her grandfather, Great-grandpa the Cursed, but can't recall what her mother did upon learning the news. What was the name of the Ohio sanatorium? How had it located the family after so many moves west? What was his official diagnosis? What happened to the letter? The body?

The details are forgotten, and who can tell whether it was Finnish closed-mouthedness, immigrant confusion, or newly acquired middle-class shame that allowed Great-grandpa the Cursed to be lost in America yet again?

This is the crossroads between the official family history that exists on paper, a more authentic history that was passed orally, and a third, more potent history that couldn't be spoken and is fading.

No Tragic Mulattos in our tree, only tragic Finns.

Falling

After Mummi's death, my mother and I move to town. Michael-Vaino, a.k.a. Uncle Mike, who still lives at home, visits late in the evenings. I creep out in my nightgown to sit on his lap.

One night when I am full in the throes of adolescence, he points to the floor.

I look down.

He runs his finger up my chest and flicks my bottom lip. My lip, loose and jutting out, bobs up and down. An old trick, a child's trick.

"Got-cha!" he crows. He roars with laughter, much more so than the trick seems to warrant.

Smiling weakly, I look to my mother for direction.

She is staring at Uncle Mike, her mouth tight, eyes slitted. None of the usual gentle pity or wary tolerance.

I know he can't be drunk or high—she wouldn't have let him in. Those are the rules. So this is something else.

Each time my half-built uncle looks at me, he bursts into renewed, helpless gales.

Years later I recall the incident, the pain as sharp and stunning as the lesson of the coffee table against my nose when I was five, its taste as salty-sweet. I am grown before I finally realize, my stomach falling in disbelief the way it had that night, what he had been reacting to—the fullness of my lip. My difference, not ours.

Mangoes and Sugarcane

R. Hong-An Truong

I am ten and gathered with my girlfriends at a sleepover. We're at Barbie's house (usually off-limits to me because her parents are, in my parents' eyes, disgracefully divorced *and* remarried), a two-story suburban paradise across the street from the green field we called the 'res and across town from my family's two-bedroom apartment. In Barbie's bedroom, its walls plastered with *Tiger Beat* magazine covers, the four of us lie nestled among pastel-colored Care Bears in the waves of her flowered down comforter, flipping through glossy-covered beauty magazines and giggling at the long-legged women with perfect faces. We listen to Madonna's "Like a Virgin," not knowing what "virgin" means, eat Emily's mother's chocolate and vanilla ice cream bonbons, and drink cherry-flavored Kool-Aid without straws so it stains our lips red. We dress up in heels and tube tops, color our faces with cheap Bonne Bell makeup that smells like ripe fruit, and prance around the room to the music. I notice Barbie's round, open face, smiling, dancing. She has the face of Barbie—the *real* Barbie—framed with golden hair cut in a bouncy bob. All the boys think she is the cutest. I see Emily's long white legs kicking out beneath

273

her as she moves and sways. Emily laughs the loudest and wears the shortest skirts. Sarah is the shyest of us all and she laughs quietly, embarrassed. Her pouty, naturally flushed lips are shocking against the pale white of her skin, and all the girls at school are jealous of her.

We focus our attention on the magazines *YM, Seventeen, Teen*. We obsess about them. They are our lifeline. I imagine Emily's legs growing and growing, until she is as tall as the giraffe-sized women; I can see Sarah's lips pouting at us from one of the covers, Barbie's cherubic, sun-kissed face smiling from the pages. But we all place our bets on Emily, because she is the tallest, and hold personal fantasies at bay. "When I'm fifteen," Emily says, "I'm going to apply for *Seventeen*'s model search contest." We all nod vigorously. "Of course, you all should, too," she adds. Everyone agrees, and I avert my eyes.

The faces of the women in those magazines mesmerize me. In the June issue of *YM*, there is a young woman named Rachel, and she is beautiful. Her peachy-tanned, lightly freckled face fills the glossy page; her head is turned to the side, blue eyes squinting slightly from the sun, her bronzed mouth open and puckered, just about to bite into the frayed meat of a succulent mango. I wonder what it is like to be her—to be Rachel with strawberry blonde hair and blue eyes and have millions of people focused on full, colored lips, biting into a tender mango dripping with juice.

❧

The burning sun darkens my skin by the minute and the adobe houses stare blankly at me in the quiet August heat as I sit sipping lemonade on the back of my parents' faded gray Oldsmobile parked in the carport. One month new to Arizona, I am bored because it is hot and there are no kids to play with. Then, two boys on gleaming silver BMX bikes whiz by without hands on their handlebars, making slanty-eyed faces, laughing and shouting, "Ching chong!" in the thick, still air that makes the words hang, suspended for a moment as I casually flip my finger up at them. I get up and go inside the house. It is hot inside, too, and I stand in front of an oscillating fan, feeling the sweat on my body cooling into a wet bath. Humming my voice into the fan in fluctuating octaves, I decide that I hate Arizona.

I am thirteen, staring at a mirror in my room, and I decide I want a new face. My older sister, Quynh, who is seventeen and very mean and angry at the world, wears makeup, and I envy the way her face comes to life with those electric colors—glittering blue shades her eyelids, purple tints her curled black eyelashes, and shocking, shocking pink glosses her full lips. She even frosts and perms her thick, straight black hair—strips like gold tossed around her head. My mother, on the other hand, wears no makeup, doesn't even *know* what an eyelash curler is, and believes that pure black is the only possible hair color for Vietnamese women. Quynh sneaks through our bedroom window at night to visit boys; I know this and my mother does not.

I love lipstick. It is a secret of mine, secret because my mother would never let me walk out of the house with it on my face. "Young girls like you shouldn't wear makeup," she lectures me in stern Vietnamese. "It makes you look cheap." I lie stomach-down on my mother's bed as she gets dressed for work at one of her jobs as a waitress at the local Chinese restaurant, China Boy. On her dresser, on a small, silver tin holiday tray made for cookies, sits a glass jar of Oil of Olay, a bottle of Tresór perfume, a tube of red lipstick that she only wears on special occasions—like Christmas midnight mass—and a half-dozen or so black pencils for lining her eyebrows. My mother twists open the lid to the jar of Oil of Olay, dips two fingers into the soft pink cream, and rubs it in slow circular motions around her cheeks, chin, and forehead. Her face shines, and I cringe, remembering that an oily shine in your T-zone is top on the list of facial "trouble spots" as reported in last month's issue of *Seventeen*. I watch her carefully as she touches the tip of the black liner pencil to the tip of her tongue and smoothes the black crayon in a perfect thin arch along her sparse eyebrow. She performs this movement twice across each eyebrow, sprays a mist of perfume on the back of her neck, and she is done. I marvel at her emphasis on the eyebrow and nothing else, and use her face as a marker of how *not* to do my face. So I conduct my own experiments in private, rummaging through Quynh's makeup drawer. I smear tubes and palettes of color in all directions and use an oversized puff to dust my face with sparkling white powder, smothering those shiny trouble spots. The powder floats above me and around me in a fine cloud until I can hardly breathe.

I am a sophomore in high school now, and my mother and I are tired enemies. She is a nag, and I don't know what I am. She yells at me about dirty dishes left in the sink and my face and hair that no longer look Vietnamese. When I look in the mirror, I see crooked lips, almost gray, and thin, small, flat eyes. So I slather ultramatte cocoa lipstick on my lips and tweak my eyelashes to stick straight up in order to make them look longer, rub my eyelids so my small creases seem bigger, try not to blink too much, and hold my eyes open wide to make my eye sockets look deeper. I clump mascara on my eye-lashes and wear dark, smoky shades on my eyes, and my mother says I look like a whore. I figure as long as I look like a beautiful *white* whore, it is perfectly acceptable, so I buy dark-burgundy lipstick to go with the other makeup. I want to be blonde, but since I hear horror stories about peroxide mak-ing your hair fall out, I color my hair Flamingo Pink with Manic Panic hair dye.

It's a Friday night and I want to go out; I want to leave the house. I kick my little sister out of our bedroom, get dressed in ripped fishnets, black combat boots, a miniskirt, and t-shirt, and stay out of sight until I hear the loud, intrusive honk of my friend Brianna's boyfriend's truck. I slip through the darkened, quiet hallway to the living room only to find my mother, in her bare feet and house clothes, standing at the door. "Just where do you think you're going? And what are you wearing?" she asks me in Vietnamese. "I did not say you could go out tonight," she says slowly, forcefully. "You have not cleaned the bathroom this week, and you will not leave the house looking like that."

I shout at her, "You never let me do anything!" I walk toward the door.

"Disrespect!" my mother shouts back as I start to walk past her, and I see her taut, pained face, her small eyes wrinkled at the corners in anger. Her tongue is clenched tightly between her teeth in pure frustration, a habit she's had since she was a child and a sure sign I have gone too far.

I am lying on the couch in the living room, staring up at the ceiling fan turning slowly above me. Sunlight is coming through slits in the vertical blinds and hitting the dust that is falling, slowly, down upon me. Today is Saturday, a good lazy day—no arguments, the house is clean, and I have no plans to leave the house, which makes my mother happy. She is sitting at the end of the couch massaging my feet with her small, rough hands, cracking my toes and making me squirm. She is telling me about Viet Nam. They are not the war stories today, but the ones about the smell of fresh sugarcane and her marriage proposals: one from a wealthy Buddhist, one from a man who drank too much, and one from my father. "I had a lot of *ban trais* when I was young, you know," she tells me. I try to picture my mother young, but it is difficult because she talks about those days as if they are mythical ones. My mother's beauty and youth are as distant as Viet Nam itself.

With one arm folded across her chest and one arm up, tapping a slender, smooth, red nail-polished finger against the side of her cheek, the woman in the black cosmetic frock peers over diamond-studded glasses, looking at me quizzically. We are at the mall, a most detestable place, on the top of my list of things and places to avoid, in fact, like copious amounts of chocolate and the Fourth Avenue Carl's Jr. on Saturday nights. But I am in San Diego with the rest of the girls from the tennis team, and I have no choice but to spend the entire day at the Fashion Valley Mall. Julie, the team manager, has somehow convinced me to get a free makeover at the Clinique counter.

The makeup woman is middle-aged, with pale, velvety skin, big teased hair dyed platinum blonde, baby-doll eyelashes that brush against her reading glasses when she blinks, and black-berry lip liner that skirts the outer edge of her lips. I can tell she spent careful time putting on her face and she just loves make-up. I mean, makeup is this woman's *life*. I am annoyed by the whole process—I roll my eyes and laugh—but privately I won-der if this is it, if I could be made up so much that I simply lose my Asianness—my face—completely.

The Clinique woman looks amused as she begins to test shades of color on the back of her pasty, white hand, look-ing down through her glasses, eyes squinting, to examine the liquid foundation skin colors. I'm thinking, Sweetheart, you've got it all wrong, perhaps this isn't such a grand idea after all. But I let her get on with it because it feels kind of good to be pampered.

Julie and a handful of other girls stand around me as I sit on the stool. They bend over the counters, walk back and forth from one vanity mirror to the next, talk over each other and through each other and at each other, gushing over the variety of colors of eye shadow, twisting open tubes of tester lipstick, rubbing rouge on their cheeks, and spraying perfume in small wet patches on their wrists and forearms. I watch them as they smear on layers, watch them in fascination as their faces are revealed, as they open up, and reach closer to some picture, some image, some ideal face I have seen before many, many times. I close my eyes and their voices grow dis-tant. I can feel the soft bristles brushing back and forth across my cheeks, my eyelids, my forehead, and I imagine the landscape of my face as disparate segments, slowly being concealed, closed up—the smooth, flat expanse of my eyelids smothered beneath eye shadow, the round fullness of my cheeks manipulated by harsh, defining strokes of pink blush, the soft weightlessness of my short, sparse eyelashes shackled by chunks of inky mascara.

The Clinique woman grabs my chin between her thumb and index finger, cupping my face and craning her neck backward, then abruptly turns my head to one side, then the other. She lets go and leans in close. Her face is inches away; I can hear her steady breathing and smell her thick perfume and see the soft, tiny pores in her face. I try to imagine, without a mirror, what I look like; maybe it's the fluorescent lighting or the chaotic noise of department store voices and the *click click click* of heels against floor tile, but I cannot, for the life of me, picture how I look. I imagine the parts of my face again, and I recognize my eyes, the hue of my skin, the shape and contours of my face, all betraying my Asianness to those who see me as something that stands for that person I call me. I am all that and more, I think to myself. I am all that and more. I am my father's nose, my mother's eyes, my grandfather's eyebrows, my grandmother's height, my aunt's cheekbones; I am history and I am Vietnamese first-generation American raised on pop magazines and stories about the war.

"Close your eyes," the Clinique woman says. "Almost done." Eyes closed, I am thinking about the invisibility of a face, how flashes of tiny bright lights replace my own image. I can't see but I can hear, still hear her breathing close to my face, my breath that is familiar, louder than hers, and the sound of my lips rolling pressed against my teeth smearing lipstick, lips cracking open, and the final, hard ("Gently, now," she tells me) resounding smack. I open my eyes to a shiny silver hand mirror and I am laughing. I am laughing and I can't stop.

"What's wrong?" Julie is asking me. "You look great, really great! I'm serious! What's the matter?"

A snapshot of my mother in my hand: She is staring at me, head cocked to the side, mouth slightly open. A dark blue scarf is wrapped around her head and neck and tied in a knot beneath her collarbone, like the old village women in Viet Nam she would tell me about. But she is not an old village woman—she is my mother, and she is beautiful a few days after giving birth to my little brother. I am thinking of the sweetness and smells of Viet Nam when my mother cooks.

Vietnamese people drink sugarcane juice like Americans drink Coca-Cola. In the fields, sugarcane stalks are tall and strong with long green leaves, trunks split in two parts by round knobs in the middle. You can buy it fresh from the market, a sturdy bit of stalk right in your hand. The skin is thick and must be peeled with a small hand knife in order to get to the juice. Ripe sugarcane is brown, and you must rip off the strings of its flesh with your teeth, chew hard, suck the nectar, and spit out the tough meat that is left. The smell of sugarcane, *mía,* is like honey, sweet and sharp.

Blonde

Amy Meissner

The windswept knoll in California where I grew up still crowns in memory like a grassy head—a whorl of parched, hip-high weeds—with a chaplet of black scrub oak, blackberry bushes, and a winding irrigation canal gathering at its base. The property overlooked ranches and orchards in Ophir Valley, and although I haven't seen it from that angle for twenty-five years, I imagine people still look wistfully up at its stable perch and wonder what the view is like from there. On clear days, we could see the Marysville Buttes standing purple in the distance, and I used to think they were the same height as our little hill. Maybe another doublewide trailer tucked its skirting into one of those folds and faced ours miles away; maybe another girl had a thinking rock where she sat in the middle of a grassy space and stared into the valley below. While some children probably would have enjoyed the idea of a mirror image on another hill far away, I didn't like to think about her. I knew my opposite would want to scream or run or jump or sing when I just wanted to sit quietly and think. She would be loud and smart and know her twelves' multiplication table; she'd have a taste for teasing and not know when to stop.

She'd figure out how easy it was to make me cry. So I flew kites and built towel forts with my younger sister, Karen, instead, even though her personality didn't meld well with mine, either. I thought my age trumped her blossoming sense of power and self-worth, but even when we were six and three, or eight and five, moving across that landscape in a blonde-twinned blur, Karen managed to hold her head higher.

We learned to recognize the waxy glaze of poison oak after decorating a mud pie with the leaves and clawing at the rash spreading up our arms. We watched our mother kill a black-and-orange snake with a pitchfork in our driveway, and when I saw snakes after that, I thought about the way my mother's blonde hair swung into her face as she jabbed and jabbed at the ground. And both of us knew the before-we-were-born story of our parents hauling two Brittany spaniels out of the canal where they'd been swept off and deposited against the debris guard miles away, nails stripped to the quick from clawing at the cement banks. When our mother sent us out to play, she watched our golden heads from the window to make sure we didn't crest the hill and dip out of sight. She trusted our memories of all we'd seen, and that our own fears would keep us safe.

Our Swedish mother was rooted to those fifteen American acres through the soil in her prolific gardens, her fruit trees, rows of corn, and squash-filled vines, and little rattled her except for the occasional call asking if the property was for sale. A stern "no" always ended the discussion, but she'd tremble at the built-in kitchen table afterward. The calls came during the week, when my dad was working and living in Nevada for five days at a time, and I used to think she was afraid someone would drive up the long gravel driveway and fight to come into our house while he was gone. I imagined pushing my dad's brown recliner against the front door or standing in my bedroom window, flinging pencils and books and sharp toys to make intruders leave. She admitted to me, when I was six or seven, it frightened her when somebody wanted something that was hers.

Karen and I kept three dolls on a shelf in our bedroom, and I think now, I wouldn't have hesitated to throw the first two cheap Southern belles out the window to protect my mother and the land she'd claimed so far from Scandinavia. We didn't know much about quality dolls when we'd first received them—they didn't move or sit, just stood primly in full, ruffled skirts. Other girls collected expensive dolls, off-limits for play, with porcelain faces and tinkling hands, certificates of authenticity, and costumes copied from history books. Not us. We explored beneath hoop skirts, tried to peel away rubber shoes, inspected cotton bloomers, theorized into which orifice, exactly, the dolls' metal stands disappeared. We thought they were beautiful at first, overlooking the apple-shaped Styrofoam heads and flat-painted eyes, lips pursed into a bright pink heart, the startling absence of noses; we never mentioned the hands, cramping like wire claws, because we were so smitten with the matching parasols they held, even if the umbrellas were permanently shut; we forgave the blonde curls glued into ringlets that could never be replaced once pulled undone.

A third doll came from a family friend sometime afterward. I don't remember if it was mine or Karen's, or if we were meant to share, but when I think of the doll even now I sense the residue of conflict associated with her arrival—a kind of fire-spitting presence sidling up to our two pretty girls on the shelf, a life force I'd never known before and which I became instantly aware I didn't have. A Spanish flamenco doll, she stood proportioned and poised with castanets in each slender hand, a lovely upturned chin, sultry lips, smoky eyes, and hair swept into a dark bun crowned with roses. Her dress's satin bodice molded to her breasts and hipbones, flaring into a bell of red and black flounces that dragged like a frothy wake behind graceful red shoes. And unlike the two wobbly Southern belles, who tipped onto their heads if the wind hushed the curtain into our room, she had weight and balance and stamina. She strutted all day on our shelf, dancing circles around those frigid blondes, yipping and clacking and pushing them to be something they didn't yet know how to be.

❦

Newcastle Elementary was a country school filled with ranch offspring and foothill kids whose parents commuted to Sacramento or Loomis, some families so large it seemed like brothers and sisters spread from kindergarten into the eighth-grade classroom. When I think about it now, I can't imagine Karen and I were the only towheads dropped off at the curb, but my memory forms a sort of liquid uniformity pooling in the dip of land where the school sat, and we slid into it like amber beads of oil. It doesn't matter the size or color of the population; any oddity will always be fair game to the hand-ful of children who thrive on finding the weakness in others. My sister, maybe because she was younger and tougher, learned to jibe in the last word and elbow her way through a crowd, stomp her heels to be noticed and heard. But I kept my back to the wall, my skin as thin and translucent as my hair, too quick to blush and cry at nothing more than a cross-eyed look.

One morning, I accidentally slipped into wooden-soled clogs for school—nobody else in my class wore shoes like these in 1979. Even though I'd fought so hard for the tennis shoes my mother was convinced would suffocate my feet, I'd forgotten about their squeak and new-rubber smell during the morning rush. I didn't notice how I clicked down the hallway outside of the third-grade classroom until Scott Byers—a boy with eyelashes I sometimes thought about touching and skin I know now could have been Latino or Native American but thought then simply looked warm and smooth and tan—pointed and asked, "Are those *Dutch-person* shoes?" I looked at the red-and-white-painted clogs a Swedish great-aunt had sent and stood paralyzed, deciding whether or not to correct him on the country of origin—people always lumped together Sweden, Norway, Switzerland, Holland, Finland—tell him these shoes were painted in Dalarna, that they were special, and certainly not *Dutch.* Instead, narrowing my eyes for effect, I told him to shut up—such forbidden words at home I thought they'd have some kind of power here. Scott instantly shoved me into the wall and said, "No, *you* shut up, you white-headed mule," then walked away. I trembled through math class and lunch and thought about my mother's only fear, but I knew I wasn't shaking because someone wanted something that was mine. I shook because I lacked the confidence to protect it from being destroyed.

Maybe his had been a legitimate question and I'd been too defensive and vulnerable; I'm sure he forgot the incident, but three days later, lying in my bed and staring at the flamenco dancer, I repeatedly snapped my fingers and imagined the perfect response: "No, *you* shut up, you brown-butted jackass." But after so many days, or even minutes, a comeback loses velocity. Even at eight years old, I knew this. So I stared at the back of Scott Byers's head for the rest of the year, just waiting for him to call me a "white-headed mule" again, but he never did. Instead, he picked on brown-haired Jill Metcalf—the girl with the built-in swimming pool whose father was a pilot at the Sacramento Airport, the girl with the permanent tan lines on her shoulders who knew how to make a fast purple bruise on any boy's arm, the girl who gave my little sister an Indian burn on the forearm after school once and then called her a crybaby. Twenty-five years later, and my sister and I talk about this—*God, remember that girl, Jill?*—and Karen is still incensed that someone would pick on a kindergartener, and I am still ashamed I never did anything to protect her. Instead, I'd just demanded she stop crying and walked her somewhere else to wait for my mother to pick us up. If I'd been a different child, a flamenco dancer maybe, I would have smacked Jill and told her to leave my sister alone. Karen would have done it herself had I let her, but I forced her to stand there with me like one of those stale blonde dolls instead, biting the inside of my cheek.

The dolls stayed on the shelf for the handful of years we lived in that mobile home. Even now, the trailer reminds me of some kind of doll—a big brown lady curtsying in a white aluminum dress, her back door wedged against the hill, the living room drapes drooping like lids. The California sun beat onto the shelf, and while the flamenco dancer was spared— red and glossy and smart enough to temporarily curtsy into the shadows—the light leached color from the blonde dolls' dresses so the ruffles faded, brittle and papery. One day, I realized my doll's organza dress was half green, half yellowish white. I can still feel the fabric on my fingertips, grinding into a gritty powder. It's a feeling that spread across my own body, but one I could never explain beyond a kind of guilt for not being happy with what I had, for what I should have been thankful for; it's a kind of loneliness that never made any sense, since I was surrounded by trees and grass and cats on the bed and by people who loved me.

It started in the mornings, an unnamable fear that had something to do with going to school but more with leaving the house. I'd sob into my bowl of cereal—that hiccupping, suffocating crying that leaves a stomach flipping until you can't breathe and the only thing that makes you feel better is throwing up. If you do, then you get to stay home. A trip to the school nurse could have the same effect. Years later, I would hear terms like "separation anxiety" or "childhood depression," and weigh these against what my mother diagnosed as "a highly sensitive child" or "shyness" or "afraid of not pleasing the teacher" or "an overachiever" or the infamous "those kids are just making fun of you because they're jealous of your pretty hair." I'll never know exactly what was wrong with me or why I felt so insecure. I know my mother looked for a child psychologist for a while, probably wondered how to pay for such a thing, but I don't know if this would have been the answer. Maybe it would have given me too much attention of the wrong sort. Maybe I would have learned a language that was too adult, too analytical, too self-absorbed, too soon. Instead, she did what she knew: She sat on the couch with me for hours when my dad was away, teaching me how to embroider, then crochet, watching me loop and pull, loop and pull until I'd stitched a seven-foot-long yarn chain I kept coiled in a red Folgers coffee can. I wonder sometimes if she thought she should have done something different, or more, but it seems that redirecting my emotion into something endless and useless, then snapping a round plastic lid on it, was the right thing to do.

In 1980, my mother started planning a six-week trip to Sweden to visit her family; I'd been twice, Karen once. Grandma Alice, my dad's mother—a woman who insisted we always wear our shoes inside the house and seemed vague about her English and Irish descent when I asked after learning what the word "nationality" meant—shook her head like she'd done each time before. "That *hair*," she said. "Those girls are targets." She told my mother stories of kidnappings and white slavery, explained how unsafe it was for a woman to travel alone with two little girls, described the men who lurk in airports—not to catch a plane, but specifically to steal children like us whose mother turned her back: *All it takes is one split second.* But my dad couldn't fly to Sweden just to protect us. He couldn't leave his family's water-well-drilling business, abandon his weekly commute over the Sierras and into Nevada, turn his back on that kind of responsibility, take time away from building a future just so he could visit in-laws who spoke a language he didn't understand. My mother never fought Grandma Alice, never fought my dad; she just planned more silently for travel, making sure my sister and I always linked moist hands with her in public. Meanwhile, her family grew older and older every year she waited. Sometimes she received an overseas call with news of someone's death, and she would walk out onto the knoll in front of our trailer to stare at the green and gold patchwork in the valley, blonde hair whipping against her face, arms holding her own waist.

After finding a box of tumbled romance novels in Grandma Alice's basement once—women's hair hanging long and blonde, breasts bulging from pirate dresses or harem tops, bodies twisting, eyes closed, and mouths gasping open at the feet of dark men—I thought this must be what white slavery looked like. *Listen to me, Ingrid, first thing they steal are those little towheads. You'll be in a foreign country. No one will help you. Better to keep them right here, safe in the United States. Maybe I should travel with you girls.* But Grandma Alice didn't understand that in Scandinavia, we weren't anything special. Once we hit the crowds in the Copenhagen airport and then went on to Gothenburg, we didn't stand out anymore. My mother wouldn't have lost us because we were different; she'd have lost us because we were the same: a sea of towheads, all blending together. I sometimes wonder what would have been more terrifying—losing your child in an unfamiliar landscape or losing your child in a place where every child looks like yours, at every turn? At Sunrise Mall in Sacramento one afternoon, I grabbed the wrong person's hand and walked clear around a penny-filled fountain until I heard my parents calling. If they hadn't missed me, I don't know how long I would have held on to a stranger or just how far he—or she—would have stolen away with me. I don't remember unclasping that shadowy hand or looking into the person's face, but I remember turning and running full speed toward my mother, who knelt with arms outstretched.

My mother would tell me, years later, she thought Grandma Alice's true fear was that my mother would take Karen and me to Sweden and decide never to come back—as if the fact her son had married a foreign woman lent an uncertainty to their marriage, a tendency to grab small children and flee, reasonless, for a homeland. Perhaps she'd offered to come along to make sure we flew home to California again, but the thought of my petite Grandma Alice sipping coffee, thin legs crossed and toes pointed in canvas sneakers, at a table full of husky, sock-footed farm Swedes trying to feed her cookies and cake still seems unlikely.

I thought if I snapped fingers and stomped heels, I'd find some kind of power to change the things I thought were wrong. My dad being away so much was wrong; anything that made me look different was wrong; having a foreign mother must have been wrong; being shy and insecure and transparent blonde— all were wrong, and these things lurched and brewed into one stewed mess until I couldn't separate one from the other. At the beginning of a parent volunteer day, I stood in the pebbled courtyard at Newcastle Elementary, looked at the ground, and through clenched teeth said, "Mom, just don't talk Swedish to me anymore. Okay?" I imagine now what her face must have looked like at that moment, at first rosy and open, then dense and quiet, soft hair feathering from her temples.

My mother used to sew long peasant dresses in browns and oranges trimmed with cotton ecru lace, and she wore knee-high boots the color of pumpkin pie. When I asked once, she promised I could have the boots when my feet grew big enough, and she polished every little scuff to keep them looking new. I used to try them on, zip that luxurious inseam zipper, and feel where her pinkie toe had worn a bulge in the leather. She wore the boots one Halloween, with a dress, a floppy felt hat, and an old mink stole someone had given her—the first little mouth an adjustable clip fastening to the last little tail. She curled her hair, applied rouge and bright lipstick. It was a last-minute costume, a surprise when she emerged from the bathroom, but an identity that still seems fraught with some kind of emotional need: For that one night, ringing doorbell after doorbell with a plastic-masked bunny and a gray polyester squirrel, she got to be "the rich lady."

But that day in the courtyard at school, I told her to erase her language and all remaining homeland in this new country, closed the filter of culture between her and her firstborn, spun and yipped and snapped, wielding a power that was stronger than both of us. I have to imagine her face now, years after I said this one thing to her, because as soon as the words spilled out, I turned and ran into the classroom so I wouldn't have to look at her. I imagine she stood there long after I'd run away, and in my mind it's the rich lady I see, mink stole and floppy hat, sobbing like something priceless had just been wrenched from her.

I should have worked harder to protect her feelings—but this is an adult's voice. I had no way to know at eight or nine what my responsibility to her culture was or that it was my heritage as well—that it was mine to claim, or that I would someday want it desperately. I was tired of kids asking me, "Hey, do you speak *Sweden* or something?" A woman once asked my mother if she was fluent in Swiss. The mothers on the PTA board consistently called her "Heidi," or "Hildie," or "Inga," since they could never remember her name, Ingrid. She moved through this with grace, sometimes gently correcting people, forming a globe in midair with spread fingers to show at what latitude she grew up, but just as often she smiled with a closed mouth, her nostrils flaring slightly. I'd started snapping back to kids, "No. I don't speak *Sweden*. Do you speak *America*? Duh."

There is something about a child's white flaxen hair that gives people the unwritten authority to palm it, to reach and search for a kind of perfection in something so rare, as if touching it, like cupping a woman's pregnant stomach, will re-create some lost connection with innocence. For a child with a shyness that is starkly worn and painful, hair like this becomes a symbol of something for the taking, a reason to shrink away from anyone who reaches for it. I still feel like no one would believe me if I said it had been a burden.

I wanted Cherokee braids—long and black and shiny-thick falling down my back with feathers blowing from the ends—but my braids looked like white rat tails, and my mother said if I poked chicken feathers in my hair I'd get mites. I wanted cornrows tipped with bright plastic baubles clicking behind me when I ran, but the rubber bands alone were too heavy, slid off, and were soon lost. I couldn't keep any flower in my hair when I twirled and stomped heels in the middle of the living room unless I faked it with a shoulder tuck to the ear while snapping castanet fingers over my head. Plastic barrettes slipped and slipped until they hung like something given up. All I wanted was a tough scalp—one that didn't flush pink when I got embarrassed and call further attention to the red-faced child with white eyebrows.

My mother kept a comb in her purse to straighten our hair in public, tamping the electricity with her palm. People beamed at us, murmured, whipping their heads around as we walked past. Sometimes it made me feel important, but most of the time it made me want to cover my eyes or tuck my face against my mother's hip.

After Karen tried to make a gum necklace and sacrificed chunks of her hair in the process, our mother stopped trimming our bangs in the kitchen and took us to a real beauty parlor. Women wearing tight perm rollers and plastic ponchos hurried from all corners of the salon to cluster around our pumped-up chairs and touch our hair with the backs of manicured hands. "Women pay big money to have hair this color. You girls are so lucky. Aren't they lucky? Their hair is just like silk." But it didn't feel like luck. *Here's something for the taking. All it takes is one split second.* Karen loved the attention, even with her recently hacked hair, but I cried the entire time. Women said things like, "Oh honey, it'll grow back!" But I cried because Tony—the hairdresser in skin-tight jeans, a blousy unbuttoned shirt, and an enormous handlebar mustache—pretended to cut off my ear with his scissors. He said he would add it to his "collection of little-girl ears" at home— he had all colors. I spent the entire haircut staring at my flushed cheeks and wobbling chin in the mirror, imagining a shelf of ears on special stands. Mine would be the blonde one.

While my father rarely attended school functions, he sometimes made Friday evening talent shows or spaghetti dinners, although I imagine him road-worn and exhausted, moving from truck to shower to freshly ironed shirt as if still under some kind of pavement-humming spell. I stood in a line at Newcastle Elementary with him once and noticed how the other kids didn't seem so big in the shadows of their parents. Having him there made me feel bigger, though. Complete. I loved his Irish Spring soap and Old Spice aftershave and wore him on my arm like a mustached red and gold dance partner, my chin held high.

He ran his fingers through the back of my hair while we waited in line, and I shooed him off, although I didn't really mean it; I thought this was his way of telling me how much he'd missed me all week, and I didn't want him to stop, even after his fingers caught a little snarl and my hair stretched until it snapped. I pictured my hair glinting like gold, a gentle puff against my neck as each strand fell into place, the electricity building and crackling in my ears. I squelched a proud smile as we stepped in unison toward the door to the cafeteria, but eventually felt the red creep into my face and scalp, tingling against his fingertips when people turned to look at us. I waved my hand behind my head again, grazing his knuckles. "D-a-a-d!" But he didn't stop.

Spinning on slick plastic soles, I balled my fists to make a goofy scolding scene, like a little shrew with her lip stuck out—I'd make all these people in line think I was tough and didn't like what he was doing. Hide how good it felt to have him there with me, back from work, back from the desert, back from muddy drill rigs and greasy dinners and breakfasts alone. That spin stays with me like a slow dizzy wheel. I see his face through fringed bangs, the ends of my pageboy whipping into my eyes. He smiled with an open mouth and raised eyebrows, rocking a little on his toes as if he'd been waiting for me to turn around the entire time, and then I see his hands in his pockets or thumbs hooked through belt loops or palms up with shoulders shrugged as if to say, "What could I do?" The man who stood beside my dad in the line—fine blonde hairs still clinging to his cocked fingers—was someone I'd never ever seen before and would never see again.

As we grew up, Karen became more and more like the flamenco dancer, and I didn't understand why *she* got to be so fearless. My mother scoured the hillside for her one afternoon, screaming and calling her name after she'd snuck down to the canal, "just to see." While I retreated further and further into myself, Karen burst forth all snapping fingers and waving arms, hands on hips for family photographs, questioning why she should smile nicely when a tongue or an open mouth had such a better effect. I started hating the flamenco doll. I thought Karen knew how to dance in gritty circles because of her, leaving me paralyzed and staring into nothingness because I was too afraid to do anything else. I opened the Folgers can and stretched my crocheted yarn chain across the floor of our bedroom to separate her from me, not because I hated her, but because I was jealous of her strength.

The two other dolls left nothing better to aspire to; I didn't want to be what they offered—a belle, a translucent princess, a rich lady. Karen had long ago dismantled the ringlets on hers, discovered the bald patch beneath the saucer-shaped bonnet of lace and tulle, taken the doll outside to play beneath the hydrangea bush. My play was more subversive. If I stuck a thumbnail into my doll's squeaky head, it left small crescent-shaped pocks. I lifted her ringlets and spread silent marks, like little hidden lesions.

In Karen's recurring childhood dream, a witch comes out of the spigot on the side of the mobile home when she tries to turn on the water; before the witch can steal her, I swoop out of the sky and we both fly away. In my recurring dream, Karen falls through a plate-glass window in an old-time saloon because a gang of older boys suddenly lets go of the baby blanket she's fighting for; when she turns to look at me, she is missing an eye because I was too late reaching her. I had this dream when I slept on my dad's side of the bed when he was working in Nevada, so I had to stop sleeping there and stay in my own room. I thought lying on his pillow and smelling him gave me nightmares—that somehow falling into the hollow his body left behind made me the family protector. At this, I thought I would always fail, even if I was quick enough or confident enough to pick something up and hurl it at the enemy, keep what I loved from being wrenched away.

At least in Karen's dream, I save her. Some part of her must have believed I could. In the end, it's up to us to figure out how to protect ourselves, whether it means keeping a tight hold on the things other people want or just finally giving them up and dancing off. Years later, Karen shaved her head—said she wanted people to see *her,* not her hair, long and thick and golden, but always more bronze than mine. Everyone still wanted to palm her buzzed scalp though, touching her more than ever before, so she'd grow her hair back, then shave it, then grow it back again, rinsing with henna for the gloss and the red, highlighting the color that already emerged so naturally. I realize how it must have been easier to be the younger child during the time our dad disappeared over the mountains every week, to not take on the need to protect our property from strangers, protect our father from the fragility of having little girls, protect our mother from ourselves. Maybe all those years ago, sitting beneath the hydrangea bush disrobing or scalping her doll, even then, she knew how to fully claim what she owned even if it meant destroying it completely first.

☙

Less than two years ago, my sister and I stood on a windy Newcastle hill after Grandma Alice's funeral. Karen had covered her bald head with a stocking cap and wore a scarf trailing on the ground behind her; my hair was less than an inch long, razored into severe tips. An elderly woman approached us and after a hello and exchange of sympathies, she dropped her eyes and shook her head. "You girls," she said, "don't you know? Your hair is your crown of glory. What a shame." Then she walked away. Neither of us had words or the velocity for a response. Days or years later, I still wouldn't. What can you say? I don't know if Karen would even remember the incident if I asked her about it now; I'm sure the comment slid off as easily as that scarf she kept tossing over her shoulder. I immediately got that old powdery feeling again though—a brittleness I thought I'd snapped a lid on long ago, but that seemed to have just been a temporary slip into shadow. That windy day, I should have protected my sister, myself. I should have held my hands in the air, at least fumbled for those lost castanets, clacked or yipped or stomped. I should have tried to point to the place on the globe above my head that day, on that bare hill, and showed the world where I thought I belonged.

Notes

Mirror

Information about the White House meeting between Eisenhower and Warren came from NPR, *All Things Considered:* "Brown v. Board of Education, Part II." Broadcast December 9, 2003.

The quote by John Lewis was taken from "Crime Stories of the Century" by Angie Cannon and Kate V. Forsyth, published in *U.S. News & World Report,* December 6, 1999.

Information in the final section, including details about Emmett Till's death and the interview with J. W. Milam, came from "Looking at Emmett Till" by John Edgar Wideman, published in *Creative Nonfiction* 19 (2002): 49–66.

The suggestion that the picture in Bo's wallet was of Hedy Lamarr came from *Death of Innocence: The Story of the Hate Crime That Changed America* by Mamie Till-Mobley and Christopher Benson (NY: Random House, 2003).

An Apology to Althea Connor:
Private Memory and the Ethics of Public Memoir

hooks, bell. *Bone Black: Memories of Girlhood.* New York: Henry Holt and Co., 1996.

Mura, David. *Where the Body Meets Memory: An Odyssey of Race, Sexuality & Identity.* New York: Anchor Books, 1996.

Acknowledgments

Above all, I must thank the brilliant women whose work fills these pages. You have been a joy to work with and have created such a beautiful book.

This book would never have come into being without the support and assistance of many people. Thank you to Leslie Miller, for believing in this project and taking a risk on a focused and passionate (but not-so-experienced) writer; Moin Hussaini, for his inspiring and thought-provoking emails; Hari Chandra, sometimes-agent, sometimes–copy editor, and always-friend, for his enthusiasm and fine critical eye; Rachel Cohen, Sailaja Sastry, and Arnold Krupat at Sarah Lawrence College, for their input and guidance.

Thank you to Raj and Rakhee Makhijani, my parents, for their unrelenting encouragement—in everything I do.

And lastly, to Jay Suresh. Thank you for making me a better writer and a better person.

About the Contributors

Faith Adiele is author of *Meeting Faith* (Norton), a memoir about being Thailand's first black Buddhist nun; writer/narrator of *My Journey Home* (PBS), a documentary about growing up with her Nordic American mother and traveling to Nigeria as an adult to find her father and siblings; and editor of the forthcoming international anthology, *Coming of Age Around the World* (The New Press). Her work appears in the Seal Press anthologies *Women Who Eat* and *A Woman Alone.* A former diversity trainer specializing in dialogues among Africana peoples, she currently teaches literary nonfiction at the University of Pittsburgh and travel writing at various summer programs.

Ana Chavier Caamaño is a freelance writer and graduate student in creative writing at San Francisco State University. She is currently at work on her first novel. Her recent work has appeared in *Cipactli*, the journal of literature and art for Raza Studies at SFSU. She frequently travels to her homelands of South Dakota and the Dominican Republic to visit her families.

Judith Chalmer is the author of a book of poems, *Out of History's Junk Jar* (Time Being Books). She is the creator of a dance narrative with oral histories, "Clearing Customs/ Cruzando Fronteras/Preselenje," about the lives of immigrants in central Vermont, and is author and performer of "Don't Go In There!" a one-woman comedy on racial and ethnic consciousness in central Vermont. She is cofounder of a women's interracial dialogue group that has met for three years in central Vermont. Her essays have appeared in *Celebrating the Lives of Jewish Women* (Haworth Press), *Urban Spaghetti, RAGU,* and other journals.

Theater columnist for the *East Bay Express* in Berkeley and a regular contributor to *Kitchen Sink* magazine, Chicago native **Lisa Drostova** has been firmly ensconced in San Francisco since 1991. In her spare time, she belly dances with the troupe Djun Djun, teaches aikido to kids, and glues things together.

Karen Elias became deeply committed to doing antiracist work after attending the 1981 National Women's Studies Association Conference, Women Confront Racism. She has taught English and gender studies at a variety of universities. Her work has appeared in *Anima, Conditions, Escarpments, Sinister Wisdom,* and *Thirteenth Moon.* In addition, an essay titled "Two Voices from the Front Lines," coauthored with Dr. Judith Jones, was published in the anthology *Race in the*

College Classroom (Rutgers University). In 2001, she received a Pennsylvania Council on the Arts grant for her memoir in progress, tentatively titled "White Bodies."

Now that she has retired from her job as a professional student, **Toiya Kristen Finley** finds herself in the predicament of being a freelance writer and editor, stuck back home in Nashville, Tennessee. While she was still in school, she founded the journal *Harpur Palate* and served as its managing editor and fiction editor. She enjoys writing and reading in a lot of different genres. Her fiction has appeared in or is forthcoming in *Fortean Bureau, Mota 2002: Truth, Paterson Literary Review, NFG,* and *H. P. Lovecraft's Magazine of Horror.* Her nonfiction has appeared in *Aim* and *Full Unit Hookup.* She received her PhD in literature and creative writing from Binghamton University in 2003.

Patricia Goodwin grew up in an Italian American neighborhood outside of Boston. She was the first in her family to finish high school and go on to college. She graduated *cum laude* from Salem State College in Massachusetts. In the early days of the natural foods movement, she created and taught educational programs for the East/West Foundation. She is currently a writer and a publicity agent for artists and independents. She promoted Women in the Arts, 2003, which raised funds for HAWC (Help for Abused Women and Their Children). In addition to her nonfiction, which has appeared in publications such as the *Boston Herald,* the *Boston Globe,* the *Record American, American Express OnTime, AAA Horizons,* and the *Salem Evening News,* she has written two books of poetry, *Marblehead Moon* and *Java Love.* Her novella, *When Two Women Die,* was recently published at the Muse online. She is currently working on two books of poetry, "The Phenomenon of Day" and "Atlantis." The essay in this book was excerpted from her novel, "Sexual Memories." She lives with her husband and daughter in a historic seacoast town in Massachusetts.

Randi Gray Kristensen teaches writing with themes in African diaspora culture to first-year students at George Washington University. She holds an MFA and PhD from Louisiana State University, and is completing a cross-cultural study of black women's writing, "Rights of Passage: Maroon Novels by Black Women Writers," focusing on works by Toni Morrison, Paule Marshall, Maryse Condé, and Toni Cade Bambara. She is also completing a postcolonial mystery novel, "Capital Crimes." She serves on the board of the African American Women's Resource Center and organizes writing retreats to Jamaica (www.naturalsouladventures.com).

A native of Chicago, **Mary C. Lewis** has been a writer and editor for twenty-seven years. She is the author of *Herstory*

(African American Images), a nonfiction book about teenagers. She has contributed to *Sleeping with One Eye Open* (University of Georgia), *In Praise of Our Teachers* (Beacon), and *Encyclopedia of the Harlem Renaissance* (Facts on File). "The Teach-In" is from a memoir supported by an Illinois Arts Council fellowship. She offers editorial assistance via www.e-writingcoach.com.

Amy Meissner spent twelve years as a clothing designer in the United States and Canada before moving to Alaska in 2000 to pursue a new life and career. She recently completed an MFA in creative writing at the University of Alaska, Anchorage, where she has been the assistant editor at *Alaska Quarterly Review* for three and a half years. She balances time as a writer and time as an artist, having finished her fourth illustrated book for children, and is soon to begin a fifth and sixth with publishers in the United States and Canada. Excerpts from her memoir collection, "A Quick Turn of Soil," have been published in the literary magazine *Crazyhorse* and in the anthology *Far From Home* (Seal Press). "Blonde," published here, is the third piece from this collection.

Colleen Nakamoto lives in the San Francisco Bay area, and was a Rosenthal Emerging Voices Fellow of PEN Center USA West. Her work has appeared in *ONTHEBUS, Spillway, Rattle,* and *Moving Pictures.*

Nnedi Okorafor-Mbachu is a journalist for Africana.com and a technology columnist for the *Chicago Sun-Times'* sister paper, the *Star* (the column is called "Nnedi on the Net").

She received her bachelor's degree in English/rhetoric from the University of Illinois, Champaign-Urbana, and her master's degree in journalism from Michigan State University. She is currently working on her PhD in English at the University of Illinois, Chicago. She recently won third place in the Hurston/Wright Awards for her story "Amphibious Green." She received honorable mention in *The Year's Best Fantasy & Horror* (14th Ed.). Okorafor-Mbachu's short story, "Windseekers," was a finalist in the L. Ron Hubbard Writers of the Future contest. She also was chosen to present her master's thesis paper, "Virtual Women: Female Characters in Video Games," at the 2001 Association for Education in Journalism and Mass Communication convention. Okorafor-Mbachu has also previously been published on USAToday.com, Pointcast. com, Essence.com, and the Student Advantage Network Online. Her short stories have appeared in the following literary journals: the *Women's International Network Magazine, Margin, Moondance Magazine, Shag, Umoja, Strange Horizons,* and *The Thirteenth Floor.* In 2001, her story "Crossroads" was published in *The Witching Hour Anthology* (Silver Lake).

Wendy Rose is the author of several volumes of poetry, including *Now Poof She Is Gone* (Firebrand), *The Halfbreed Chronicles* (West End), and *Bone Dance* (University of Arizona).

Esmeralda Santiago is the author of the memoirs *When I Was Puerto Rican* (Addison-Wesley), *Almost a Woman* (Perseus), and *The Turkish Lover* (Da Capo). She has also written a novel, *América's Dream* (HarperCollins), and has coedited two literary anthologies featuring Latino writers. Her books are required reading in schools and universities throughout the United States and in Puerto Rico. Ms. Santiago wrote the screenplay for the PBS Masterpiece Theatre film version of *Almost a Woman*, which won a Peabody Award. Her essays and opinion pieces have appeared in major newspapers, including the *New York Times* and the *Christian Science Monitor,* as well as in mass-market magazines. She has also been a guest commentator on National Public Radio. In addition to her literary achievements, Ms. Santiago has designed and developed community-based programs for adolescents, and was a founder of a shelter for battered women and their children. Ms. Santiago serves on the boards of organizations devoted to the arts and literature and is an impassioned spokesperson for supporting the artistic development of young people. She graduated from Harvard University, earned an MFA from Sarah Lawrence College, and is the recipient of three honorary degrees.

Sejal Shah is a fiction writer, poet, essayist, and teacher of writing. She is the 2004–2005 writer-in-residence and CSMP Scholar at Luther College in Decorah, Iowa. Previously, she taught creative writing at Mount Holyoke College and at the University of Massachusetts, Amherst, where she earned her MFA. She is the recipient of an Academy of American Poets prize and fellowships from the New York State Council for the Arts and Blue Mountain Center. Her writing has appeared in many journals, including *Massachusetts Review, Indiana Review, Pleiades, Meridians,* the *Asian Pacific American Journal, Hanging Loose, Catamaran,* and the anthology *Contours of the Heart* (Temple University). Currently, she is completing a collection of short stories, "Ithaca Is Never Far," and a series of nonfiction essays exploring South Asian diasporic identity. You can reach her at sejalshah1019@yahoo. com.

Devorah Stone's passion for art led the way to a visual arts degree from the University of Victoria. Her true love for writing surfaced later, after marriage and three children. She has published articles on bread baking, donuts, buffalo meat, online confession booths, dancing hamsters, penguins, snowflakes, women rabbis, weightlifting, high school graduation, Pokémon, and life on other planets. A former Web reviewer for the Encyclopædia Britannica online guide, she has published articles, fiction, and reviews widely in

Inscriptions Magazine, Verbatimag, FolksOnline, Highlights for Children, Chatelaine, Papyrus magazine, *Amateur Chef,* and *Straight Goods,* among others. She is the host of the Historical Fiction Forum.

Anita Darcel Taylor received her MFA from Bennington College and has written a forthcoming collection of personal essays on mental illness, race, and identity. Her personal essays have been published in anthologies and literary journals. Currently, she lives in Washington, D.C.

R. Hong-An Truong is the documentary arts educator at the Center for Documentary Studies at Duke University. A photographer and writer, she is actively working on issues that involve youth, education, and racism. Her work includes coordinating youth programs that use photography, audio production, and writing as a lens for young people to learn about community issues, media activism, and self-representation. Truong's photographic work has been included in exhibits organized by Chambers Fine Art Gallery in New York, the Godwin-Ternbach Museum at Queens College, and the International Center of Photography, among others. In 2002, she was awarded a residency at both the Center for Photography at Woodstock and the Visual Studies Workshop in New York. She is the coeditor of a special issue of *Southern Exposure* on Asians in the South, which will be published in 2005.

B. Lois Wadas is a director, playwright, poet, and performance artist based in New York City. Her first full-length play, *Woman to Woman,* was first performed off-Broadway and then at the Harlem Theatre Company. She twice moderated "A Round Table of Women Writers," aired on Manhattan Neighborhood Network. Wadas is an active member of the International Women Writers Guild. Her work has been widely published in the United States and Canada. Her work has also been featured online at *KUMA, LiterateNubian,* and *Timbuktu.* As a psychotherapist, Wadas conducts workshops and discussion groups in New York, California, and Washington, D.C. She developed and conducts "The Good Breast" and "Ms. Right," relationship workshops sensitive to both culture and gender. As an adjunct professor, Wadas directed Ntozake Shange's *For Colored Girls Who Have Considered Suicide When the Rainbow Is Enuf* at SUNY Stony Brook. She recently produced and directed *Woman to Woman* at the Harlem Theatre Company, and she mounted "WomenWording," a choreopoem, in March 2004. In February 2002, Wadas appeared on HBO in the *Vagina Monologues.* She also appeared on Queens Public Television in September 2003 in Autumn Magic, commemorating 9/11. She is in private practice in New York City.

Traise Yamamoto is associate professor of English at the University of California, Riverside. She is the author of *Masking Selves, Making Subjects* (University of California). Her essays, poems, and fiction have been published in *Breaking Silence* (Greenfield Review), *Premonitions* (Kaya), the *New Republic, Signs, Poetry Northwest,* and elsewhere.

About the Editor

Pooja Makhijani is an essayist, journalist, and writer of children's literature. Her byline has appeared in the *New York Times*, the *Village Voice*, the *Star-Ledger*, the *Indian Express*, *Time Out New York*, *NY Arts Magazine*, *India Today*, and *Time Out New York Kids*, among others. Her first picture book, *Mama's Saris*, is forthcoming from Little, Brown & Company. Currently at work on a collection of essays, she lives with her husband in New York City.

Selected Titles from Seal Press

Colonize This!: Young Women of Color on Today's Feminism edited by Daisy Hernández and Bushra Rehman. $16.95, 1-58005-067-0. A diverse collection of some of today's brightest new voices, taking on identity, family, class, and the notion that feminism is one cohesive movement.

Cunt: A Declaration of Independence by Inga Muscio. $14.95, 1-58005-075-1. An ancient title of respect for women, "cunt" long ago veered off the path of honor and now careens toward the heart of every woman as an expletive. Muscio traces this winding road, giving women both the motivation and the tools to claim "cunt" as a positive and powerful force in the lives of all women.

Pilgrimage to India: A Woman Revisits Her Homeland by Pramila Jayapal. $14.95, 1-58005-052-2. This eloquent and spirited book weaves together perceptive commentary on contemporary issues with Jayapal's own profoundly moving journey of self-discovery.

Secrets and Confidences: The Complicated Truth about Women's Friendships edited by Karen Eng. $14.95, 1-58005-112-X. This frank, funny, and poignant collection acknowledges the intricate relationships between girlfriends.

The F-Word: Feminism in Jeopardy by Kristin Rowe-Finkbeiner. $14.95, 1-58005-114-6. An astonishing look at the tenuous state of women's rights and issues in America, this pivotal book empowers young women to change their situations.

Without a Net: The Female Experience of Growing Up Working Class edited by Michelle Tea. $14.95, 1-58005-103-0. The first anthology in which women with working-class backgrounds explore how growing up poor impacts identity.

Seal Press publishes a variety of nonfiction and fiction by women writers. Visit our website at www.sealpress.com.